SELF-

G

Ma

OTHER SELF-CATERING GUIDES PUBLISHED BY CROOM HELM

Self-catering in Portugal
Carol Wright

Self-catering in Spain, the Balearics and the Canary Islands
Carole Stewart with Chris Stewart

SELF-CATERING IN GREECE

Mainland and Islands

Making the most of local food and drink

Florica Kyriacopoulos and Tim Salmon

CROOM HELM
London & Sydney

For Eleni

Croom Helm Ltd, Provident House, Burrell Row,
Beckenham, Kent BR3 1AT
Croom Helm Australia Pty Ltd, Suite 4, 6th Floor, 64-76 Kippax Street,
Surry Hills, NSW 2010, Australia

British Library Cataloguing in Publication Data

Kyriacopoulos, Florica
Self-catering in Greece mainland and islands
1. Cookery, Greek
I. Title II. Salmon, Tim
641.3'009495 TX723.5.G8

ISBN 0-7099-1589-6

Typeset in ITC Souvenir Light by Leaper & Gard Ltd., Bristol, England
Printed and bound in Great Britain by
The Guernsey Press Co. Ltd., Guernsey, Channel Islands.

Contents

1

Introduction

Eating is an important part of Greek life. It is above all a social event, an occasion for family and friends to relax and renew or maintain contact with each other in that noisy, cheerful, informal, warm, physical way that seems so typically Greek to the outsider. The food itself seems almost incidental. It gets none of the close analytical attention the French, for example, give to every course. It almost seems forgotten, scattered over the table, much of it being shared in communal plates, while the diners talk, laugh, call down the table, tousle a child's hair and not uncommonly end up with a hearty sing-song. The message is: food is the occasion for a good time. And the traditions of Greek cooking reflect this.

Greek cuisine is tasty and spicy, but not at all complicated or fussy in either its preparation or presentation. There is no formal succession of courses. Meals begin with a selection of shared starters, often very simple to make and heavily flavoured with garlic. Main courses are vegetables cooked with lashings of rich pure olive oil or stuffed with rice and minced meat, casseroles of meat and vegetables combined or grilled meat and fried or grilled fish served simply with a generous squeeze of lemon juice. Baking is usually reserved for the choicer and bigger fish, grilling for the best meat cuts, with the exception of lamb, which is the favourite Greek roast. Desserts of the pudding and pie variety do not feature in traditional Greek cooking at all. Meals end simply with a selection of the beautiful, colourful fruit that grows so abundantly in the country.

With the exception of some of the vegetable and savoury pie recipes, most of the recipes included in this book require little in the way of complicated preparation, which means that even if you do not feel inclined to spend your holiday in the kitchen, you can still enjoy the experience of eating in a very Greek way. In fact, if you bought a small, cheap barbecue as we recommend (see page 76) and stuck to grilled meat and fish, starters and salads, you could eat extremely well and cheaply, while hardly doing any cooking at all!

Our assumption throughout this book is that you are interested in the country, the people and their ways, no matter how different they may be from yours. And Greek ways, concerning food and many other aspects of life, are very different and individual. It seems an obvious thing to say, but people often do expect abroad to be somehow the same as home, and when it is not, they are disappointed, frustrated and even angry.

Greece lies on the edge of Europe, not just geographically, but culturally as well. Historically, it has long looked East quite as much as West and for four hundred years – some parts until the end of the First World War – it was under the dominion of the Moslem Turkish empire. Although many Greeks are understandably not very keen to acknowledge it, the Greek way of life was very deeply affected by this experience – from the bureaucratic attitudes of civil servants to the nation's eating habits. Turkish coffee is an obvious example of this influence, though the Greeks now call it Greek coffee. But a large part of the cuisine is Turkish and Levantine in origin too, as are many of the words for different foods. *Briám* and *imám bayaldí* are particularly obvious examples, and there are many others: *tzatzíki*, *keftédhes*, *yiaóurti*, *moussakás* and so on. Although the main purpose of this book is to provide practical information, we have tried also to give some insight into what is different about the Greek way of life, at least in so far as things to do with food are concerned.

In addition to the recipe section, which is big enough, without being overwhelming, to keep you busy back home as well as on holiday, you will find a mass of information not easily obtainable elsewhere.

We have included accounts of all the fruit and vegetables, meat, poultry and fish, dairy produce, herbs and so on that are commonly produced in Greece, with details of the times of the year they are available, the uses they are commonly put to, an indication of their price and geographical distribution. There is information about shopping, where to go, what to get and how to do it; and, for when you go out, a detailed description of the different kinds of place you can eat and drink at.

2

HOW TO USE THIS BOOK

The recipe section will tell you what you can make, how to do it and what ingredients you need. The first five chapters on fruit and vegetables, meat and poultry, seafood, extras (which cover all sorts of sundries like herbs, cheese and cooking oils) and wines describe what is available in Greece, what it is mainly used for, and when and where you can buy it. Eating and Drinking Out provides a comprehensive guide to restaurants and cafés. The Glossary is a basic vocabulary of English words with their Greek equivalents, which you will find useful in shopping, cooking and going out. The Index lists all the main items mentioned in the book under both their English and Greek names and tells you where in the book to find them. The remaining sections are just as their titles suggest.

3

LOCAL FRUIT AND VEGETABLES

FRUIT

Greek fruit is a treat for anyone who comes from northern climes. Many of the beautiful, exotic things we eye longingly and hesitatingly on our own greengrocers' stalls are natives here. What is more, from June to the end of September, they are plentiful, cheap and ripe – none of your standardised bullets picked early to last the long journey to a foreign market.

In fact, if you are budget-conscious and cooker-shy you can live pretty well on a diet of fruit padded out with good Greek bread, feta cheese and tomatoes.

Apples (míla)

You can find apples all year round in Greece, although their natural season runs from September through the winter months. In summer it is wise to keep them in the fridge; otherwise the flesh quickly turns to cotton wool – *patatiázoun*, as the Greeks say: they go potatoey.

You won't see apple trees very often, for the parts of lowland Greece visited by most foreigners are too hot. They are grown mainly in the north and in the mountains, where the temperatures are cooler. The main varieties of eaters are the sweet red *bananómila* – literally, banana-apples – and the ubiquitous Golden Delicious. Best of all are the distinctively Greek *firíkia*, a small, firm, oblong yellow apple with a strong scent that comes on the market in the autumn.

A popular and simple way of serving any variety is peeled and sliced with a sprinkling of cinnamon (see page 000), or just dipped in your wine glass.

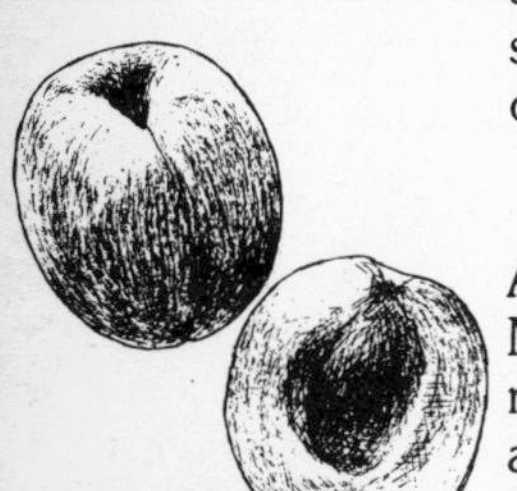

Apricots

Apricots (veríkoka)

Apricots are on sale from the middle of May to the end of July. Of the three commonest varieties, the earliest – *tsaóulia* – are the best to eat. Small, pale and heavily scented, they are also the most expensive. The hard-skinned orange *kaísi*, which appear towards the end of the season, are chiefly used for making jams, compotes and the very sweet, sticky Greek preserves – *glikó tou koutalióu.*

Bananas (banánes)

Bananas are to all intents and purposes unobtainable in Greece. The government will not permit imports in order not to prejudice the sale of home-grown produce, and the home-grown banana is small, not very tasty and so expensive that greengrocers will not buy them. The only place you ever see bananas on sale is by the roadside, where they are sold illegally at way above the recommended price.

Cherries (kerásia)

Heralds of the summer fruit season, cherries are as much prized in Greece as elsewhere. From their first appearance in the second half of May, street stalls in Athens are loaded with them and all along the roadsides in cherry-growing areas you see peasants and their children holding up great woven clusters of them to tempt the passing motorist. First on the market are the sweet black *mávra* cherries, followed in June by the firmer and slightly sourer yellow-red *petrokérasa*. The season lasts, in theory, until the end of August, but outside the more expensive shops in Athens you won't find many after mid-July.

One of the most improbable Greek cherry enthusiasts is the Pindos bear, a few of whom still survive in the mountains of the north-west. We have been told several times by mountain villagers that hungry bears have damaged their trees in spring in search of the fruit!

Figs (síka)

Fig trees grow all over the Greek countryside, both cultivated and wild. Every village garden has two or three, and you see them growing out of dry stone field walls and abandoned huts and by springs. As long as they don't obviously belong to anyone, you can help yourself to the fruit. But, be warned: not for nothing is syrup of figs a well-tried, traditional laxative.

Figs

Though there is an early green variety available in mid-July, the main fig season is August and September, when the sweet, fleshy *vassiliká* figs come on the market. They ripen very quickly and are best bought, or picked, while still mainly green. As they turn purple they split and the wasps get at them. If you are picking wild ones, make sure they are not full of little white maggots.

Grapes (stafília)

Greek grapes are cheap, delicious, full of sun and in season from late June until Christmas. There are numerous varieties of white, black and pink. Best of all is the *soultaniá*, on the market from the end of July until mid-October. It is a white, sweet grape, that comes in two varieties, large and small, both of them seedless. It is the grape the Greeks use for making sultanas. It goes particularly well with yoghurt.

Lemons (lemónia)

Lemons are the most widely used fruit in

Greece. Sliced or quartered they are served with a multitude of dishes from soups and pulses to fried or grilled meat and fish, the juice to be squeezed liberally over your food. So don't be surprised at a taverna to be presented with a plate of quartered lemons before any other food has appeared on the table!

The commonest use of lemon juice is in making dressings for green salads, where the Greeks invariably substitute it for vinegar, considering it much healthier. It is also used for basting, mixed with oil and a pinch of oregano, and as the basis for oil and lemon and egg and lemon sauce.

Abundant throughout the year, lemons are at their best in November and December. They are sold by the weight and very much cheaper than at home. The idea of buying them one at a time would seem utterly ludicrous to a Greek.

Lioquats/Kumquat (móusmoula)

A name to conjure images of silky girls and sultans' tables, though the appearance of the fruit, unfortunately, doesn't quite match it. Golden yellow, round and slightly smaller than an apricot, it often looks battered and blemished. The taste, however, is distinctly original: yielding, refreshing, mildly acidic – you feel it along the border of gums and teeth! Most people prefer to peel them, and you certainly need to watch out for the large hard stone. The season is short: mid-May to end of June. A lot of trouble for a small reward, you might think. Just try them.

Melons (pepónia)

The two commonest varieties of melon are the early small, round Cretan melons and the much bigger, rugby-football-shaped variety that last through the summer months. Greenhouse-grown, the

Cretan ones come on the market as early as Easter. They are sweet and tasty, but a good deal more expensive than the summer variety. Both have a wet mush of seeds at their centres, which can easily be scooped clean with a spoon. With the bigger variety, the flesh is harder and needs to be cut from the rind with a knife. It is particularly good – aside from the glorious combination of colours – chopped into chunks and combined with the scarlet flesh of the watermelon, or served as part of a general fruit salad. Both kinds are best slightly chilled.

How to choose one without being fooled by your almost certainly wily greengrocer? Well, there is no absolutely foolproof method, unless you are very experienced. Forget about the colour. Smell and touch are the guides. Its back end, i.e. the one opposite the stem, should be soft to the touch – not squidgy, just soft. And it should give off a distinctly melony smell. Don't be embarrassed about nosing it. The greengrocer will be impressed rather than horrified.

Nectarines (nektarínia)

A hybrid-child of the peach and the plum and surely the most successful man-made fruit. Only introduced into Greece five or six years ago, its popularity is already threatening the traditional peaches. The Greek ones are particularly good, with skin as smooth as the proverbial baby's bottom, coloured with a becoming maidenly blush, and flesh that is slightly firmer but just as juicy as a peach. Locally produced, with little distance to travel to market – there is no excuse for the shopkeeper slipping a bullet in your bag here. The season is mid-June to September.

Oranges (portokália)

Homegrown oranges are available all

year round, although the best season is either side of Christmas. Of the three main varieties, Merlins are best for eating. The redder *sangouínia*, which last up to about Easter, are particularly good for making juice. The summer Valencia oranges tend to be rather dry.

Crete and the Peloponnese are the chief orange-producers, where whole stretches of country are lush with the thick, dark foliage of the orange groves. And if you travel this way in springtime, you'll see enough orange blossom to launch a million brides. The air is almost unbearably heady with the scent for miles around.

Peaches (rodhákina/yermádhes)

There are two kinds of peach in Greece. *Rodhákina* are the smaller. Slightly pointed and with a pronounced scent, they are tastier but more expensive than their rivals, the larger, rounder, fleshier and more orangy *yermádhes*. They share the same season, from July to September. Refrigerated peaches are still available in October, but their taste has gone off noticeably by then.

Pears (ahládhia)

The first pears on the market, around the middle of June, are the small, rounded and heavily-scented *kondóules*. They are the tastier, but won't keep in the fridge like the larger and later *kristáli* variety. An inexpensive fruit in Greece.

Plums (korómila/vanílies)

The two varieties are on the market in June and July. *Korómila* are rounder and slightly smaller than *vanílies* and greenish in colour. *Vanílies* are reddish-purple, very juicy and rather like nectarines in taste.

Pomegranates (ródhia)

An insignificant tree hardly taller than a man, the pomegranate produces a brilliant red flower. As it fades the fruit grows out of it, a spectacular red and gold bomb the size of a large orange. If left to ripen on the tree, the hard rind-like outer case splits scattering the thousands of crunchy little seeds embedded in the bitter flesh inside – just like a fragmentation bomb, and this in fact is where the grenade gets its name from. They are devils to clean, which is probably why they are not grown commercially. The edible part are the little pellets containing the seeds. A sharp, refreshing and original taste – they are best eaten slightly chilled and mixed with other fruit in a salad, although real aficionados will enjoy cramming them greedily into the mouth in handfuls! The juice is said to be a good remedy for diarrhoea, and is sometimes administered to children for that purpose. But if you can't ingest them in any form at all, you'll find that grouped in a bowl pomegranates make a very attractive winter decoration.

Pomegranates

Perhaps because of the fleshy colour and the fact that they are full of seeds, pomegranates seem to have been associated with fertility in some parts of the country. In some villages in the Peloponnese, for instance, a bride would smash a pomegranate on the door-post as she entered her new husband's house, then scatter the bits in four directions to make the sign of the Cross. This was the signal for the celebrations to begin, with a song sung by the bridegroom's people, that began, 'We have tricked you and taken your pomegranate' – i.e. the bride herself.

Prickly pears (frangósika)

Not a commercial crop at all, but the fruit

of a wild, spiky cactus whose great bat-shaped 'leaves' you see all over the Greek islands and southern parts of the mainland. The fruit, which turns yellow and red when it ripens in October, grows like inverted pears all along the edges of the bat-like 'leaves'. Despite its unpromising exterior, it has a rich, sweet and most unusual flavour. But be extremely careful peeling the fruit. It is covered with tiny hair-like prickles, and if you get any in your mouth it will be several days before you can eat anything comfortably again.

Strawberries (fráoules)

An introduced fruit, strawberries are not commonly found in Greek households. They are produced mainly in the north of the country and come on the market from June to August. Expensive at the beginning of the season, the price drops way down by mid-July. The Greek way of presenting them is interesting too: they leave them to marinate in lemon juice and sugar (see page 136), which accentuates and refines the flavour.

Tangerines (mandarínia)

The first tangerines ripen at the end of October, and the season continues through the winter months to about the end of March. Clementines are the earliest variety: small, sweet, seedless, and rather more expensive than the commoner, loose-skinned, traditional tangerine. As with most other citrus fruit, the north shore of the Peloponnese and Crete are the major producers, though the island of Chios is also renowned for its *mandarínia*.

Watermelons (karpóuzia)

Trucks piled with them, pyramids of them stacked by the roadside: great green footballs striped with paler green, one always slashed like a wound to show the ripe red flesh inside ... Watermelons are the symbol of summertime in Greece. And they are not just beautiful to look at. When properly ripe they are deliciously juicy and refreshing. Cut them, like other melons, in quadrants or smaller segments, slice the flesh from the rind, and clean out the tiresome little black seeds. Again, they are best eaten slightly chilled. Whole, they will keep for two to three weeks, but once cut, they need to be refrigerated. Make sure the temperature is not too low, however, or they half-freeze and spoil.

Choosing a good one is rather a hit-and-miss affair for most people, although from July onwards (the season lasts from June to the end of September) you can be fairly sure they are ripe. Weight is supposedly the chief criterion of ripeness. The lighter, the riper – contrary to what you might expect. But as they weigh up to 30kg (65lb), it is pretty hard to tell. (See Weights and Measures for explanation of equivalents.)

Colour means nothing. And the pale patches of discoloration often found on one side are simply where the monster has rested on the ground. Don't be alarmed by the freak weights. Average sizes are 5 to 10kg (11 to 22lb) and prices are as low as 10 drachmas per kilo – in other words, a remarkably good buy.

VEGETABLES

Eaten raw as salads, stuffed, boiled, fried or casseroled – and always with a generous application of olive oil – vegetables play the dominant role in traditional Greek cooking. If preparation of some of the more intricate recipes seems time-consuming, this is because vegetable dishes are often the main course.

Until recently the population was predominantly rural and poor. People did not eat meat, because they could not afford it. Besides which, the mountainous terrain and dry climate make it impossible to raise livestock and cereal crops on anything like the scale common in more northerly European countries.

While these factors may hinder the development of large-scale industrial farming, they are positive advantages as far as quality goes. Greece produces a wide and exotic range of vegetables, which thanks to small-scale production, limited use of chemical fertilisers and plenty of sunshine are cheaper, tastier and more wholesome than most of their standardised counterparts in other countries.

The few imported vegetables are considered luxury items. Besides being expensive and obtainable only in the more sophisticated markets of Athens and Thessaloniki, they hold no place in traditional cooking and have not been included here.

A number of new vegetables have been introduced into the local producers' repertoire in recent years, such as Webb's and iceberg lettuces, mushrooms, and avocados, which are now grown under glass in the southern part of Crete. They are, however, still considered a novelty and remain expensive by comparison with traditional varieties. They are therefore not commonly used in Greek households.

In the past vegetables were always entirely seasonal. And for this reason many dishes were associated with a particular time of year and often with some special tradition like Lent or Easter. Nowadays, with the aid of greenhouses, most varieties are produced all year round. While this does make it possible to cook your favourite dishes throughout the year, it remains a fact that vegetables grown under glass are never as wholesome and tasty as those grown in the open air and harvested in their natural season. They are also a good deal more expensive, costing three to four times as much as when they are in season.

So, in the general advance of what passes for progress, frozen veg are now widely available. Though obviously not as nutritious as fresh ones, they do have certain advantages. They are cheaper. They are clean and usually require no preparation before cooking. Not that this is a consideration that would interfere with an old-fashioned Greek cook's sense of duty and commitment to freshness. It could make a difference to you, though, if you're just in Greece on holiday and not keen to be slaving in the kitchen when you could be cleaving the silky Aegean. Besides, there's nothing like some good olive oil and a generous admixture of onions for livening up the blandest frozen item!

In the listing of vegetables that follows, we have given an

indication of price, season, availability fresh or frozen and a brief outline of some of the ways in which individual vegetables are prepared, cooked and served.

Artichokes (anginàres)

With their spiky leaves and tight scaly heads, artichokes look like the vegetable equivalent of the armadillo. The edible part is the head – the only bit you'll see on the greengrocer's counter. Despite the unpromising exterior, the soft, compact flesh of the heart and the inner leaves are extremely tender. And these are the parts used in the characteristically Greek artichoke recipes, although you can perfectly well eat the base of the outer leaves, dipped in a vinaigrette sauce, as the French do.

The subtlest of the Greek recipes is *anginàres a la políta*, a speciality of the old Greek community of Constantinople/Istanbul, with artichokes cooked in oil with carrots and potatoes. In other recipes, artichokes are cooked with broad beans and peas, or boiled and served with oil and lemon, and occasionally used, as in *moussakás*, as a substitute for aubergines or eggplants.

Artichokes in Greece are homegrown, chiefly in the Corinth-Argos region of the Peloponnese and on the island of Crete. The most popular variety is the small globe artichoke, on the market from September to June, considerably cheaper than in northern countries.

Aubergines/Eggplants (melitzánes)

Widely used in Greek cuisine, aubergines or eggplants are now available all year round. During their natural season, which lasts from June through November, they are among the cheapest vegetables on the market. The rich purple variety with a taut glossy skin are called *fláskes*. Here, swollen with summer heat, they often reach the succulent proportions of small

Aubergines

marrows. They are, however, rather bitter and should be well doused with salt before cooking (see page 120). Their principal uses are in making *moussaká* and *melitzanosaláta*, a dip of creamed aubergine.

A second variety, known as *argítikes* from the region of Argos, is less spectacular in appearance but milder and sweeter to the taste. A pale speckled purple-white in colour, smaller and more sausage-like in shape, they are mainly used in *imám bayaldí* and *papoutsákia* (see page 118) for stuffing with tomatoes and onions.

Either variety, however, can be used for making *melitzánes tiganités* (fried aubergines; see page 102), which, like fried courgettes, are served as a *mezés* with *skordhaliá* (garlic sauce).

Beans (*fasólia*)

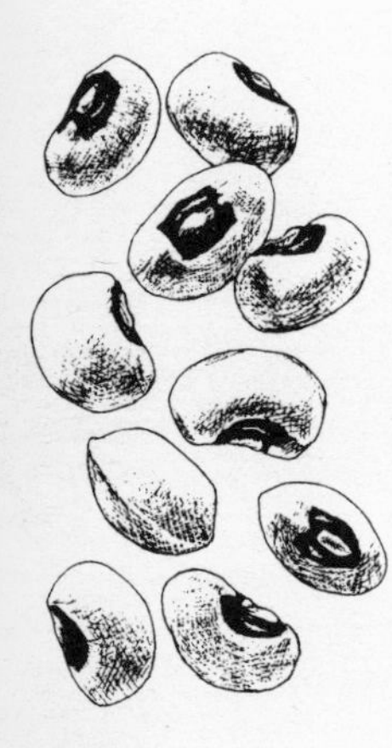

Beans

Dry beans, like the other pulses, are a Greek staple. Haricot beans (*fasólia*) are used in the popular winter soup, *fasoládha* (see page 111). *Yígandes*, a relative of the butter bean often called Giant beans, are served as a *mezés* (see page 110), while the black-eyed or *mavromátika* beans are eaten cold as a salad (see page 103).

Of the green beans, French or bobby beans (*fasolákia*), whose natural season is early summer, are cooked with lashings of olive oil to make the tasty *fasolákia ladherá* (see page 118).

Beetroot (*padzária*)

Though the variety is the same as that familiar to cooks at home, beetroot in Greece is always sold uncooked and complete with its leaves. Root and leaves are boiled separately and served cold as a salad either with an oil, vinegar and garlic dressing or with *skordhaliá*. Always cheap, they are in season from May until

October, although at their best up to the end of June.

Cabbage (láhano)

No Greek would dream of eating hot boiled cabbage. Both red and white varieties of Savoy cabbage are available, from September to the end of February. Occasionally cooked, but usually served crisp and raw with oil and lemon dressing, they provide much the most appreciated winter salad, without which no Greek meal would be complete.

Carrots (karóta)

You're unlikely to find tender baby carrots available unless it is in an up-market Athenian shop. The regular Greek carrot is a horny old root, nonetheless tasty for that, but best and most frequently used either in soups like *fasoládha* or grated in cabbage salad.

Cauliflower (kounoupídhi)

Cauliflowers are a cheap winter vegetable, on the market from November to February. Their principal use is in salads; they are boiled and served cold with an oil and lemon dressing.

Celery (sélino)

Greek celery is a smaller, thinner, bitterer plant than its counterpart at home. Probably because of the taste it is much more widely used in soups, in *briámi* and with pork than in salads. It can be found the year round, though in winter it is thicker and tougher than in summer.

Courgettes/Zucchini (kolokíthia)

Baked, boiled or stuffed the versatile courgette or baby marrow appears in Greek cuisine in many guises. To the British palate its most unexpected roles are as a salad, lightly boiled and served cold, or deep fried in batter (*kolokíthia tiganitá*

– see page 104). The weirdest description of it we have ever come across was on a taverna menu, where it was advertised in English as 'fiddlesticks in garlic sauce'! Work that one out if you can.

Available all year through, courgettes are at their cheapest and best in the summer months.

Cucumbers (angóuria)

Available throughout the summer months, cucumbers are an essential ingredient of salads and, combined with garlic and yoghurt, of the dip called *tzatzíki*.

Garlic (skórdho)

Aside from its almost universal use for flavouring in Greek cooking, garlic has long been valued for its medicinal properties. Some people even eat it raw in the belief that it stimulates the heart, eases the flow of the blood and a thousand other things. Several varieties grow wild in Greece. One of them, with a tight knob of tiny purple flowers on a metre-tall (40-in) stem, is common near the sea. Its bulb is usually half out of the ground and quite safe to eat with your picnic.

One of the most interesting and tasty uses the Greeks put garlic to is a thick mushy sauce called *skordhaliá* often served as an accompaniment to vegetables and, also, cod.

Greens, wild (hórta)

Unlike most modernised societies, the Greeks have not yet lost their links with their ancient rural roots. People, especially in the country, still go out to gather the fruits, nuts and edible plants that nature offers free. *Hórta* are one of them – a general term covering a variety of dandelions, mustards and other edible 'salad' plants. Typically after rain, you see old ladies in faded print dresses bottoms-up in the olive groves or among the thorny scrub of a hillside, stabbing at the ground, gathering these dandelions. Far from being dismissed as the food of the poor, they are regarded as a delicacy and served by restaurants as a salad with an olive oil and lemon dressing.

Leeks (prása)

Leeks are a winter vegetable in Greece, lasting through to the end of April. They are principally used in making *prasórizo*, a dish of leeks and rice, either eaten on its own or served as an accompaniment to meat, or *prasópita* – a leek pie.

Lettuces (maróuli)

Maróuli invariably means the long-leaved Cos lettuce, which hailed originally from the Greek island of Cos close to the Turkish coast. The taste is a little more bitter and the texture coarser than the traditional round lettuce. Available all year round nowadays, they are still best in nature's season, between February and May. The Greeks nearly always slice them into thin ribbons in a salad, which not only makes the leaves more manageable but helps them soak up the flavour of the dressing more effectively. Together with cabbage, *maróuli* is the main winter salad.

The last ten years have seen the introduction of a new variety, similar to ours. Cultivated around Marathon, by the sea just to the north of Athens, it is not widely available away from the capital. It is also more expensive than the Cos.

Okra (bámies)

Ladies' fingers, the old vernacular name, makes you think of something elegant and delicate. Not so the okra – it's ribbed, plump and slightly hairy, though notwithstanding this unflattering description it is one of the more highly prized

Okra

and exotic vegetables with a distinctive aftertaste. It is chiefly used in casseroles or as a *ladheró* dish. With a short season – June to September – it is never particularly cheap, though you'll pay less for it frozen.

Onions

Onions (kremídhia)

Red-skinned, a little more compact and much more piquant than ours, the Greek onion finds its way into the preparation of just about every dish in the repertoire. And liberal quantities of it are sliced raw into every summertime tomato salad – too much for some more Western taste-buds. Spring onions, on the other hand, which are available all through the winter and up to about May, are reserved for *maróuli* salad.

Peas (arakás)

Fresh peas can be found in the shops from February to April. They are also widely available tinned and frozen. The latter, more expensive than fresh ones, are packaged in three separate sizes. Most typically, they are casseroled with artichokes or tomatoes.

Peppers (piperiés)

Another spectacularly colourful vegetable, their natural season is from May to November, though they are now produced throughout the year. Of the large varieties, the green ones are used most distinctively as *yemistá*, stuffed with rice or minced meat, or baked, then served cold with olive oil, lemon and garlic as a salad. The sweeter red ones are mainly served baked, as above, or used for *toursí*. The small varieties, both green and red, can be either hot or sweet, so be careful to choose the ones you want.

Potatoes (patátes)

In Greece, as elsewhere, potatoes are a staple, as the long-suffering Greek soldiery know to their cost, and eternal complaint. They are obtainable all year round, though not in great variety. The average Greek potato is a large, misshapen-looking veteran; the small, tight, spring variety is practically unheard of. They feature in *moussakás*, *briámi*, and numerous casseroles, roasted with lamb and chicken, and as chips with just about everything grilled, meat or fish. The restaurant fried potato, it has to be said, is no match for the French version: it tends to be chunky, soggy and cold.

Spinach (spanáki)

Always cheap and readily available from August to June, spinach is used in a variety of ways: boiled, as a salad like *hórta*, as a garnish and – most typically Greek – in a tantalisingly tasty, flaky pie called *spanakópita*. Also available frozen.

Tomatoes (domátes)

Greek tomatoes are one of nature's greatest gifts. Huge, juicy, gorged with heat – you can taste the sun in them. And never mind the occasional split, blemish and irregular shape. In the shops all year round, the summer months are nonetheless far their best season. They are used in a wide variety of recipes, all the *ladherá* and pulse dishes, and often with meat. Stuffed with rice, sultanas and pine nuts (see page 122), they make the summer's lightest, coolest, subtlest midday meal. They are also the principal ingredient of summer salads, served either on their own with salt and oil and a sprinkle of onion or as part of the *horiátiki*, the so-called Greek or village salad.

4

LOCAL MEAT AND POULTRY

Greece does not produce a lot of meat and until recently the Greeks were not big meat-eaters. Because of the climate and terrain there is not the grazing to support large herds of beef cattle. Sheep and goats are the traditional livestock. Nearly every rural family used to keep at least a few sheep and goats, but for their milk, cheese and yoghurt rather than the meat. Killing a sheep to eat was like destroying a vital part of your meagre capital, something that would only be done to celebrate very special occasions like a wedding or the Resurrection of Christ at Easter. Apart from the Paschal lamb many people ate no meat at all.

This scarcity and the relatively poor quality of meat in the past have shaped the traditional Greek recipes for cooking meat. With the exception of spit-roasted lamb and chops, meat is seldom eaten on its own for its own sake. The traditional recipes are clearly designed to enhance the flavour of meat by cooking it with vegetables, herbs and spices, or to make a little go a long way by combining it with other ingredients, like bread in *keftédhes*, rice in *soutzoukákia*, or using it as a filling for stuffed vegetables. And nothing is wasted. There are recipes for using all the offal: soups like *patsá* and *mayirítsa* for using up the intestines, *kokorétsi*, which consists of various bits of offal bound up in entrails and grilled on the spit, as well as the more usual liver and kidneys.

Now that meat-eating has become almost a symbol of prosperity, a lot of meat has to be imported to satisfy the demand. Poultry, however, is mainly produced locally.

When you go to the butcher's (*hasápis*), you will find there is practically no meat on display, and certainly not the ranks of chops, legs and joints familiar in butchers' shops in northern countries. When you give your order, the butcher is quite likely to go to his fridge, select a piece of meat, chop and wrap it without you even catching a glimpse of it, so it is a good idea to make it clear you want to see what you are getting.

You will also find that the cuts are unfamiliar, or rather that there do not seem to be any cuts at all. This is because traditional Greek butchering was not really concerned with cuts, for reasons which have to do with the way meat is cooked. Though it is possible to be more specific about the cuts you want nowadays, people still most often ask for meat for boiling (*yia vrastó*), meat for roasting (*yia psitó*) and so on. This is probably the simplest way for the non-Greek-speaker to order meat too, though it does mean putting your fate in the hands of the butcher.

You order meat by the weight, except for poultry of course, which you buy by the piece. The State fixes the price per kilo (2.20lbs), according to three categories, where beef and pork are concerned. The first and most expensive comprises the best lean cuts like steak and roasts. The second comprises meat that is suitable for casseroles, like *kokinistó* (see page 132), and the third – the cheapest – meat for boiling.

Butchers are not happy about selling small quantities – less than half a kilo, sometimes even less than a kilo. This is part of the general tendency to encourage customers to buy more than they want, so you have to be quite firm about your order.

Frozen meat and poultry are also available at the butcher's. But poultry in Greece essentially means chicken. Duck and turkey are rare, imported and expensive. They hold no place in traditional Greek cuisine.

Fresh game has all but disappeared from the market as a result of serious depletion of the native game stocks by uncontrolled overshooting. A certain amount of game is obtainable in Athens – at a price – but outside you are unlikely to find more than frozen quails (*ortíkia*) and the occasional frozen rabbit. Turtle-doves (*trigónia*), woodcock (*bekátses*) and partridge (*pérdhikes*) are extremely rare outside a few game restaurants.

MEAT

Goat and kid (yídha, katsíki)

Young kid's meat is highly esteemed in Greece, indeed more highly than lamb. When it is truly young, the meat is very tender and tasty, and less fatty than lamb.

But it acquires a strong flavour and becomes tougher as the animal ages. The Greeks do eat goat, usually boiled, but if you are not used to it, you'll be safer sticking to kid. A goat could be as old as six!

Kid, like lamb, is best from December to April, although you can now find it throughout the year. A popular recipe is *katsíki ladhorígani*, prepared in the same way as lamb *ladhorígani* (see page 129). All kid is locally produced, but as the supply is limited the price is higher than lamb. Most expensive of all are wild goats, *erífia* – not often obtainable, but extremely good to eat.

Mutton (arní)

Lamb (*arnáki*) is generally the safest buy when shopping for meat in Greece. As lambing takes place in the autumn and not the spring as in countries further north, lamb comes on the market between December and April. Best of all is the suckling lamb, *arnáki gálaktos*, milk-fed and under four months old.

While all the lamb sold in Greece is domestically produced, the mutton is partly imported, mainly from New Zealand, Bulgaria and Yugoslavia. Lamb from eastern Europe is said to be very good too. The main cuts obtainable at the butcher's are leg (*bóuti*) for roasting and making *souvlákia*; shoulder (*spála*) for pot roasts and stuffing; cutlets (*païd-hákia*) for grilling and breast (*stíthos*) for casseroles. All mutton cuts are the same price per kilo.

The traditional way of cooking a lamb is to roast it whole out of doors on a spit over a pit of burning embers, as still happens with the Paschal lamb. And there are, in fact, restaurants (*psistariés*) which specialise in spit-roasted lamb (see page 87) all the year round. What comes as a bit of a surprise to the foreign visitor is that you are expected to order your meal by the weight – so many kilos of meat. Popular taverna lamb dishes are *païdhákia* (see page 129) and *arnáki ladhorígani* (see page 129). *Estiatória* (see page 85) do a number of lamb casserole dishes prepared with various seasonal vegetables, like peas, okra, beans and artichokes. A favourite spring dish is *arnáki frikasé* – lamb cooked with lettuce and egg and lemon sauce.

Pork (hirinó)

The cheapest meat you will find in Greece, pork is mainly eaten grilled or roasted. Fresh or frozen, it is available all the year round.

The main cuts are the leg (*bóuti*) for pot and oven roasts and boiling; chops (*brizóles*) for grilling on charcoal with oil and lemon – they have more taste than veal *brizóles*; and shoulder (*spála*) for pot roasts and boiling. Pork also makes the best minced meat and the best *souvlákia*.

Pork *brizóles* are standard taverna fare. Some good pork dishes to be found at *estiatória* are *hirinó me fasólia* (pork with beans) and *hirinó frikasé me sélino* (fricassee of pork with celery).

Veal and beef (moshári, vodhinó)

Most of the veal and beef consumed in Greece is imported from Germany and Holland. Besides being cheaper, it is also better quality and leaner than the home-grown product. There is, however, a certain amount of confusion about what does or does not count as veal. No self-respecting restaurant ever has anything other than *moshári* on its menu, which is always translated as veal, although what you eat looks and tastes more like beef, and often not so young as all that.

The reason is that *moshári* in Greek can mean a beast anything up to three years old, whereas the real white meat of the milk-fed calf is extremely uncommon and much more expensive. And where the calf ends, there the beef begins. So *vodhinó* proper can really be a bit long in the tooth.

The top cut, and priciest, is fillet (*filéto*). Rump (*kilóto*) and shoulder (*spála*) are used for casseroles with vegetables and pot roasts. The chops or *brizóles* are always grilled and breast (*stíthos*), the cheapest cut, is sold for boiling or pot roasting. Minced veal – often mixed with minced pork – is standard for making meatballs (*keftédhes*). *Souvlákia* are generally made from rump or leg. Veal liver (*sikóti*) is also widely available, fresh and frozen.

Commonest taverna dishes are *brizóles mosharísies* (see page 133) and *biftékia*, the Greek equivalent of the hamburger, prepared with onions and oregano. Two of the nicest *estiatório* veal dishes are *vodhinó stifádho* (beef casserole with onions) and *moshári kokinistó* (veal cooked in tomato sauce; see page 132).

POULTRY

Chicken (kotópoulo)

Chicken is eaten a lot in Greece. It is reasonably priced, widely available and generally tastier, whether fresh or frozen, than its Western factory-farmed cousin. It is usually sold whole, complete with giblets. If it is not already cleaned, you can ask the butcher to do it for you. He will also truss or quarter it for you too.

Some of the most popular chicken dishes to look out for are *kotópoulo sóupa avgolémono* (chicken soup with egg and lemon sauce – see page 110), *kotópoulo me bámies* (chicken cooked with okra – see page 127), *kotópoulo sto fóurno me patátes* (roast chicken with potatoes – see page 128), and *kotó-poulo kokinistó* (chicken cooked in tomato sauce). Chicken is also served with pasta, rice and French fries.

In recent years, frozen chicken pieces packaged by Voctas, the major poultry enterprise, have become available. And large supermarkets also sell frozen poussins, called *nanákia* in Greek.

5

FISH AND SEAFOOD

The sea and fishing have played a large part in Greek popular culture, as you would expect in a country with so much coastline and so many hundreds of tiny island communities. Though emigration, prosperity and tourism have made large holes in these traditions, the professional *psarás* – fisherman, from *psári* a fish – still exist. You see them pulling out of island harbours at dusk or dawn in their beautiful curving, broadbeamed caiques (*kaíkia*), the helmsman nonchalantly controlling the tiller with his foot, while the engine thumps its slow 'doug-doug-doug' and a string of smaller boats bounces along in the wake. Sun-blackened faces are the fisherman's hallmark, and missing limbs; for many of them still prefer a good charge of dynamite to a patient night at the nets.

And there are plenty of amateurs and part-timers too, making a little extra, supplementing the family diet or simply indulging a private passion. And they'll all tell you one thing, pros and amateurs alike. Fish are scarce; the waters have been badly overfished.

The result so far as the market goes is that prices are astronomical and the most sought-after species of fish are virtually unobtainable, because the tourist restaurants get first pick. The delicious and once plentiful red mullet (*barbóuni*) is scarcely allowed to reach two fingers' length before he ends up on someone's table. By and large the bigger fish are considered the choicest and are most expensive. They are most commonly baked, or boiled, while the medium-size fish are grilled and the smallest fried. Even the smallest, like *marídhes* (picarel), which were once dirt cheap are now relatively expensive.

Far the best place for buying fish is the Athens fish market, which, admittedly, is not a lot of help if you have come to Greece for a seaside holiday. However, do go and see it if you have time to spare. It is a colourful, raucous place, and will give you an instant panorama of who's who below the surface of the Aegean.

Outside the capital, fishmongers as we know them are more or less non-existent. Fish is usually sold at open-air markets – *psaragorá* – or on the quayside, which is the best place to go to head off the intense summertime competition. Make sure the fish is fresh. It goes off quickly in Greek summer temperatures – and should, incidentally, be eaten the day it is landed. A truly fresh fish should still have a twinkle in the eye, red gills and upward-curling tail, and its scales should not come off too easily.

Of course if you are not particular about eating only fresh fish, there are many more options. Frozen fish, including squid, octopus and all the fanciest species, are widely available at supermarkets and butchers' shops, at no more than a third of the fresh price. In our experience they are extremely good quality and when properly cooked indistinguishable from the fresh ones.

When planning a fish meal out, the place to look for is a *psarotavérna* – fish taverna. Although seaside tavernas invariably do serve fish, *psarotavérnes* make a speciality of it. Again, the Athens area is particularly good. You should be a bit wary of the renowned fish restaurants in the old Tourkolimano area of Piraeus – now called Mikrolimano (small harbour), since the Turks invaded Cyprus in 1974. The setting is very attractive, but they are expensive, and the service is not always as good as it should be. There are lots more all along the shore by the suburb of Glyfadha. Best of all would be a trip – 40 minutes on the bus – to the little port of Rafina on the east coast of Attica or to Halkidha about one and a half hours to the north where you can tuck into sumptuous displays of shellfish while observing at your feet one of the world's most puzzling tide phenomena. The current under the bridge joining Halkidha (which lies on the island of Evia) to the mainland completely reverses direction every few hours, as if a hand were tilting the seabed. No one has been able to explain why, from Aristotle's day to this. In fact, they say the great man threw himself in the water in frustration.

FISH

Anchovy (gávros)

Also called *antsóuyia* in Greek, anchovies are small fish, never more than about 20cm (8in)in length, with blue-green and silver sides. In winter they live a couple of hundred metres down, but in spring and summer they swarm close to the surface of the sea in large shoals and are easily caught. Plentiful, inexpensive and tasty, they are eaten fried, or baked, sometimes with tomatoes and onions. The head is bitter and better not eaten. They are also available preserved – and very salty – in cans or jars.

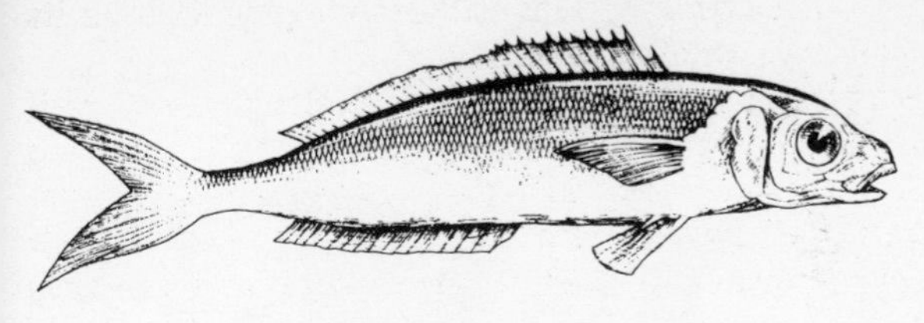

Bogue

Bogue (gópa)

Silver with yellowish tints, *gópes* are a decent-sized small fish – definitely out of the down-in-one class. Common and cheap they are generally obtainable throughout the year. Although they are not reckoned one of the classier fishes, we consider them tasty, good value for money, and an excellent buy at all times, especially in the winter months when they are fatter. They are nearly always eaten fried; it would only be worth baking an exceptionally large one.

Cod (bakaliáros)

In Greece, *bakaliáros* invariably means salted cod. Primarily a winter dish, it is fried and served with the strong garlic sauce, *skordhaliá*, or simply with lemon. Without the added piquancy of the *skordhaliá*, the taste is slightly sour.

Cuttlefish (soupiá)

Cuttlefish look roughly like a large version of squid, up to about 25cm (10in) long with eight short and two longer tentacles. The meat is rich and tasty. They cost about half the price of

Cuttlefish

octopus, and are a good deal tenderer – they don't require energetic beating, which is a definite plus. They are usually cooked with white wine and onions or with spinach.

Dentex

Dentex (sinagrídha)

One of the Aegean's most sought-after fish, the dentex is meaty, toothsome and expensive – fresh, that is. Frozen, it is a third of the price, and who would notice the difference? It can be up to a metre (40in) in length, but is usually half to three-quarters that size. The colouring varies with age; the adults are a light brown with silver-white bellies and blue spots down their sides. Available all year round, they are more plentiful in summer. They are usually cooked grilled and served with *ladholémono* (oil and lemon juice), or baked in a tomato sauce *a la Spetsióta*, after the manner of the island of Spetses.

Gilt-head bream (tsipóura)

Another excellent fish, mostly obtainable in winter, and served either grilled or baked with an oil and lemon dressing and a sprig of parsley. It is a good size too,

Gilt-head bream

between 30cm and 60cm (12in and 24in) or so in length. With grey back and silver sides, it is most easily recognised by the gold spots on each cheek.

Mackerel (skoubrí)

Mediterranean mackerel look and taste the same as those caught in the Atlantic. Grilling or baking in the *a la Spetsióta* tomato sauce is the best way of cooking them; it lightens that rather heavy, indigestible quality.

In the spring, the small, young mackerel are caught for preserving. Soaked in brine and sun-dried, they are called *tsíros* and can be bought at the grocer's. They are usually eaten as a *mezés* with ouzo.

Pandora (lithríni)

A fat half-pound *lithríni* with its tight white meat makes one of the best fish meals you can get. Rather short and deep-bellied, they are vaguely pinkish in colour with blue spots scattered along their sides. Most common in October, they are not cheap. Frozen, however, they are no more than a fifth of the fresh price. Baking and grilling are the usual methods of cooking.

Picarel (marídha)

Marídhes are tiny, like whitebait, scarcely bigger than a finger. Deep-fried in olive oil and liberally sprinkled with lemon juice, they are a favourite *mezés*. You eat them whole, in a single bite.

Physiologically they are curious little creatures. Their colour and sex varies according to their size. They are hermaphroditic, starting life as females and becoming male as they exceed 13 cm (5 in) in length! They live in shoals near the surface and are easily trawled by the broad-beamed traditional fishing caiques. They are best in winter when they are a bit fatter and have more taste.

Red mullet

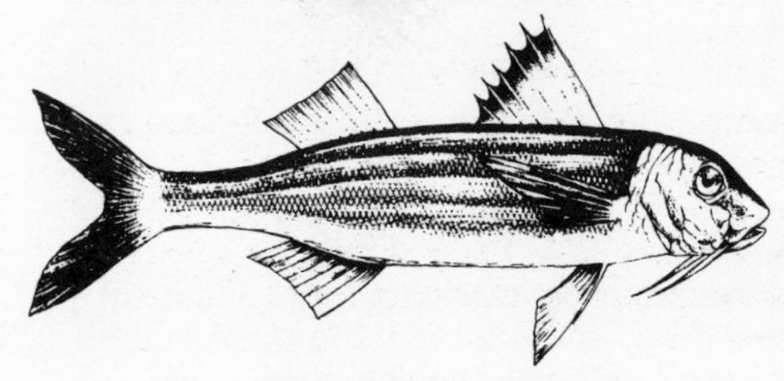

Red mullet (barbóuni)

The prince of fish, a Greek friend calls them. And they are certainly very tasty, leaving a curious sort of smoky aftertaste on the palate. Not a big fish, they are immediately recognisable by their rosy red colour, with a couple of horizontal red lines along their flanks. They used to be plentiful, but Greek waters having been heavily overfished, you can usually only find the smaller ones nowadays, and those at a price. The price, it has to be said, reflects quality as well as scarcity. They are much cheaper frozen. They are usually fried, though grilling is worthwhile for the larger ones.

Sardines (sardhéles)

Probably the cheapest and most widely available fish in Greece, canned at least, which is the way the Greeks prefer to eat them, especially to accompany the various pulses. They are available salted as well.

Spring through to October is the normal fishing season, and the standard method of cooking fresh sardines is in the oven with tomatoes, onions, pepper and parsley.

Sea bass

Sea bass (lavráki)

A big fellow, up to 1m (3.3ft) in length and 7kg (15lb) in weight, the sea bass is endowed with plenty of firm, white, light meat – with the bonus of being relatively boneless. It is eaten grilled, baked or boiled.

Red sea bream

Sea bream (fangrí)

Like its relatives, the dentex (*sinagrídha*) and pandora (*lithríni*), the sea bream is one of the tastier and more expensive fish. Up to 70cm (27in) in length, with rosy tints on back and sides and scattered blue spots, it can be cut into steaks, grilled or baked *a la Spetsióta*. The frozen version is also good, and very much cheaper.

Sole (glósa)

Ugly little customers with flat bodies and myopic eyes, they are nonetheless delicious to eat. Fresh ones are hard to find and very expensive, but they are readily available frozen, either whole or in fillets. For a small difference in price, you can get the frozen ones skinned and ready for the pan. In Greece they are usually fried with breadcrumbs or baked with spinach.

Swordfish

Swordfish (xifía)

Some 3m to 4m (9 to 13ft) long with a sword-like snout a third of its overall length and up to 300kg (660lb) in weight, the swordfish is a veritable monster of the deep, at least in the Mediterranean scale of things. They come down from the Black Sea in spring, lay their eggs in shallow water and return north again in winter. They are sliced into fillets and grilled or made into *souvlákia*, like a sort of fish kebab. The meat is very filling and flavoursome.

Two-banded bream (sargós)

Similar in taste to the gilt-head bream, the *sargós* is normally eaten baked. It is recognisable by the vertical markings along its silver-grey and brown sides. Also available frozen.

SEAFOOD

Cockles (kidhónia)

Sadly, they are scarcely obtainable any more, though not so long ago you would always see men hawking baskets of them round seaside tavernas. The Athens fish market always stocks them, and most city fishmongers will get them for you if you ask. They should always be eaten alive. The test is whether they twitch when you sprinkle lemon juice on them!

Lobster

Lobster (astakós)

In Greece, as everywhere else, lobsters are prohibitively expensive. They are much cheaper frozen, but still very pricey. Restaurants charge by the weight for them.

Mussels (mídhia)

Like cockles — they are about the same price — you get them in Athens and practically nowhere else. They are available frozen and tinned, of course, but imported.

Octopus (ohtapódhi)

It is difficult, especially in a country like Greece whose local traditions were so strong and so colourful, not to blather on nostalgically about the old days. But, once upon a time and not that long ago, octopus were far more plentiful in Greek waters. Every harbour wall and seaside rock had its horny-footed fisherman thumping his morning's catch mercilessly on the ground to tenderise it. Strings of octopus hung in the sun to dry along the café terraces. For sun-dried, charcoal-grilled octopus were — and still are when available — a favourite *mezés* to nibble at with your ouzo. In fact, we know a place where, rather than let the tradition die altogether for lack of fresh octopus, they hang up frozen ones to thaw in the sun!

Nostalgia aside, when it comes to cooking your own, there is little to choose

Octopus

between fresh and frozen. The price is similar. If anything the frozen slightly have the edge. They are always available. Though they tend to be bigger, they have already been tenderised, which saves you contracting that uncomfortable complaint, octopus elbow. The best way of cooking them, apart from the grill, and one which avoids the problem of rubbery texture, is casseroled in wine (see page 125).

Oysters

Oysters (strídhia)

If you can get them, eat them uncooked and sprinkled liberally with lemon juice!

Prawns (garídhes)

Fresh prawns are hard to find outside Athens as well as being expensive. It is cheaper and easier to buy the frozen ones. They are most often served grilled with an oil and lemon dressing.

Prawns/scampi (karavídhes)

Again, hard to find fresh and much cheaper and more widely available frozen. Serve grilled with oil and lemon or boiled and served with mayonnaise.

Sea urchins (ahiní)

Sea urchins are wicked things to tread on when you're bathing. The spines break off in your flesh and are very hard to get out. The old remedy is to put olive oil on the spot; it is supposed to make it easier to draw the spine. But, clouds have silver linings ... the chances are you can eat your tormentor. If it is black, leave it. If it is reddish, it is edible. Prise it off the rock with a knife, scrape out the soft underside, and inside the shell – if the time is right – you'll see some small crescents of orange-yellow flesh surrounded by a briny liquid. Tip out the liquid, and eat the flesh with a good squeeze of lemon juice. The taste is mild and delicate. The pleasure is mainly in the exotic appearance. No one bothers to sell them commercially any more: just gather your own.

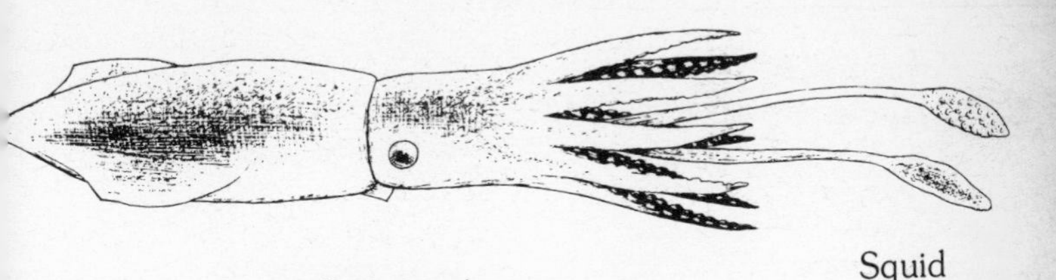

Squid

Squid (kalamári)

Deep-fried *kalamarákia* or baby squid are as much an emblem of summertime Greece as the ubiquitous watermelon. Every seaside taverna has them, and they are also very simple to cook for yourself (see page 126). The largest can be up to half a metre (20in) long, but it is best to buy them as small as you can – they are much less rubbery. Widely available frozen.

6

EXTRAS: DAIRY PRODUCTS; DRIED FRUIT, NUTS & SEEDS; HERBS & SPICES; HONEY; OLIVES; OLIVE OIL & COOKING FATS

DAIRY PRODUCTS

Butter

Greek butter (*vóutiro*), usually made from ewe's milk, leaves much to be desired. It has a strong smell and thin, rancid taste that is unlikely to appeal to the visitor's palate. Some cow's milk butter is produced nowadays, but that too compares unfavourably with other European brands. Unlike yoghurt, butter was never an integral part of the Greek diet and that, along with the fact that there are few cows in the country, probably accounts for the poor quality of the product. If, however, you cannot do without your daily butter ration, there is a wide variety of foreign makes available at reasonable prices in all but the remotest places.

Greek butter itself is best disguised with honey in a common breakfast combination called *méli me vóutiro*, honey with butter. It is the Greek equivalent of a continental breakfast, served with slices of fresh bread in most pastry shops.

Cheese

Greeks eat a lot of cheese (*tirí*), though it is usually served as a prelude to a meal, as a *mezés* with an aperitif, or during the course of a meal, rather than at the end. At the *kafenío*, if you ask for a *mezés* with your ouzo, you're likely to be given a small plate of tomato, cucumber, olives and cheese. For a long time cheese was one of the basic ingredients in the diet of most of the rural population. Today it is eaten in salads, fried as a *mezés*, cooked in spinach and cheese pies. Traditionally it was also a breakfast food in so far as the Greeks ate breakfast at all, and some people still continue this practice. It is also served with fruit.

In this section we have listed the most common or interesting varieties of cheese, along with their uses. Greek cheeses are not fine cheeses in, say, the French sense and the range is rather limited too. There are a few distinctive types, but their taste and consistency vary greatly according to their region of origin, so you would be well advised to taste them before buying. This is a perfectly acceptable practice and any *bakális* (grocer) will cut you a snippet to taste.

Féta Although it is by far the most popular and best known of Greek cheeses, large quantities of the *féta* now consumed in Greece are paradoxically produced – and more cheaply, too – in Holland and Denmark. Still, when in Greece, you might as well try to get hold of the homegrown variety.

Originally made only of sheep or goat milk, it is now made from cow's milk too, hence the considerable variation in taste. It is a white, well-salted cheese that comes in two forms: hard (*sklirí*) and semi-soft (*malakiá*). On the whole, most palates prefer the *malakiá*.

As for its uses, it is an essential ingredient of the *horiátiki* salad and provides the stuffing for *tirópita*, *spanakópita* and *kolokithópita* (cheese, spinach and courgette pie). It is popular as a *mezés* served with a sprinkling of olive oil and a pinch of oregano, and many Greeks like to eat it with watermelon.

Formaéla A cooking cheese from the Mt Parnassos region of Greece, *formaéla* comes in hard, ribbed cylinders – so hard, in fact, that it is difficult to cut. But once sliced it fries to a light golden brown colour and is soft and very tasty.

Graviéra A hard, gruyère-type cheese traditionally made from ewe's or goat's milk, though cow's milk is used as well nowadays. It is extremely expensive and, if you are not careful, can taste like anything from nothing to rubber or soap. There are numerous varieties, all known by the name of the region that produces them. Some people claim that the Cretan and Dhodhoni varieties are best. But after long experience of chewing a host of unpalatable cheeses at moments of stress and discomfort in various odd corners of the Greek mountains, we have come to the conclusion that the Lamia and Metsovo varieties are most reliable and bring most instant relief! However, let us not raise your hopes. Neither is going to be the once-in-a-lifetime experience for your taste buds.

Kefalograviéra, which is made principally in Crete, is a harder and saltier version of the same thing.

Kaséri A mild yellow table cheese made of either ewe's or cow's milk. It is also fried as a *mezés* (see *saganáki*, page 104). It used to be very popular, but something seems to have gone wrong with the quality control in recent years. More often than not, it tastes like an over-salted bar of soap. Definitely to be tasted before you reach for the wallet!

Kefalotíri Very hard and salty, it is mainly used for grating and makes an excellent substitute for Parmesan cheese with pasta.

Manóuri A soft white, inexpensive table cheese with a pleasant mild taste. *Manóuri* goes well with fruit and honey.

Mizíthra It is a soft white ewe's milk cheese that somewhat resembles cottage cheese. There are more or less firm versions of it, and it can also be bought salted or unsalted. The salted version is only used in cooking, with pasta, stuffings and pies. The unsalted is much pleasanter to eat, though a little bland. All *mizíthra* is best eaten fresh, as it does not keep well even in the fridge.

Milk

Fresh milk (*gála*) is widely available, but tastes a little thin to those of us raised on richer dairy produce. Fresh cream is confined to the towns, but long-life milk of both Greek and foreign manufacture can be found almost anywhere in full cream, semi-skimmed and skimmed forms. Long-life cream is also obtainable in the more sophisticated places. Condensed and powdered milk are universals.

Yoghurt

The Greeks make excellent cow's and ewe's milk yoghurt, far superior to any other yoghurts obtainable in Europe. This is true of both the large-scale industrial manufacturers, of whom Fage are much the best, and the local producers, whose products are usually only available in a very restricted area. The latter normally only make plain ewe's milk yoghurt (*próvio yiaóurti*), and it is invariably superior to the big brands. Don't be put off by the rather amateurish packaging, or the creamy yellow skin that covers these yoghurts — it is delicious. Cow's milk yoghurt is available plain, strained and flavoured. The strained is thicker and richer and if you don't immediately get hooked on it, you must be impervious to all addictions. A most inedible piece of paper protects the top of the strained yoghurts, so don't forget to remove it before plunging in.

Because of the closeness of their rural past, urban Greeks are still very keen on eating good country bread and fresh homemade yoghurt. So, rather improbably, on the outskirts of large towns and in villages along main roads you will find shops advertising *horiátiko psomí* – village bread, where weekend drivers stock up on the way home. These shops almost always have fresh yoghurt as well, attractively presented in earthenware bowls. As no yoghurt keeps for very long, and the homemade variety least of all, always check the 'Eat by' date, which by law has to be stamped on the packaging. At good urban grocers' and in country town dairy produce shops you can still buy yoghurt by the weight, though it tends to be sourer than the packaged varieties.

Sweetened with sugar or honey and mingled with fruit or nuts, yoghurt makes an excellent breakfast food and dessert. The Greeks also use it for making *tzatzíki* (see page 109). Although it is not a Greek practice, you can make some very tasty and refreshing summer drinks with yoghurt by mixing in a blender with chopped fruit, ice cubes, and a little honey and water.

DRIED FRUIT, NUTS, AND SEEDS

Greece produces a considerable variety of nuts, both cultivated and semi-wild, and these, along with seeds and dried fruit, play a prominent role in the nation's nibbling habits as well as in the cuisine. While some of the nuts are extremely expensive, largely because of the labour of gathering and processing them, seeds like *pasatémbo* – marrow seeds – are dirt cheap. Both are sold from street barrows by itinerant vendors, who scoop them from their trays into little cones of twisted paper of predetermined size. The barrows themselves are often interesting, ingenious homemade contraptions painted in brilliant colours.

The generic term for all these dried fruits, nuts and seeds in Greek is *xirí karpí*, and this is what you will see written above the shops that specialise in them. Not that you will be in any doubt about the kind of shop it is, for they are usually half-open to the street like stalls with great rolled-down sacks of apricots, nuts and currants standing on the floor. These places normally sell their goods *híma* or loose, but you can also get them packaged. Supermarkets generally stock both dried fruit and nuts, whereas grocers are likely to have the fruit and liquor stores (*cáva*) the nuts.

Apricots, figs and plums are all sold dried. The quality is usually first rate and the prices low. Apricots can be sour, and it is probably best to buy them by the weight so you can taste them first. Mixed with nuts they go well with drinks, or can be added to fruit salads and ice-creams.

A speciality for which Greece, and Corinth in particular, has been renowned since antiquity, is the production of currants (*mávres stafídhes*) and sultanas (*stafídhes*). They are used in stuffings, and along with pine nuts go particularly well in stuffed tomatoes and peppers. Mixed with nuts they are an excellent accompaniment for drinks, or a nourishing trail snack for walkers who do not want to be burdened with the weight of picnics. They are of course also used in cakes and fruit salads.

Nuts are listed separately below as they are more numerous.

Almonds (amígdhala)

Used in stuffings, cakes, pastries and *glikó tou koutalióu* fruit preserves, especially grapes and apricots, almonds also make a good addition to fruit salads. They are among the cheaper nuts, and are widely available throughout Greece.

The almond tree is a common garden tree, so many people produce their own nuts. The pretty white blossom which comes out as early as February is taken as one of the first signs of spring.

Almonds

Chestnuts (kástana)

The fruit of the sweet chestnut tree, which you can only find growing in the cooler temperatures of the mountains, chestnuts are used for stuffings and sold roasted on the streets in winter.

Hazel nuts (foundóukia)

Expensive, and mainly served with drinks. They also make a good addition to fruit salads.

Marrow seeds (pasatémbo)

Pasatémbo — meaning 'pass-the-time',

from the Italian – are salted and roasted marrow seeds. They are very cheap and popular, particularly with the young and with movie-goers. They are nearly always on sale outside summertime open-air cinemas. To eat them, in the cinema at least, you split the flat pod between your teeth, lick out the green seed with your tongue and spit the empty shell over the heads of those sitting in front of you. Luckily there is no circle in open-air cinemas.

Pine nuts (koukounária)

Pine nuts are the very small, white, pellet-like seed of a particular type of pine tree. As they are not grown commercially, the nuts are hard to get and very expensive. They are sold, packaged, in very small quantities and used only in cooking – for stuffings and with pilaf. They are an almost essential ingredient of stuffed tomatoes and peppers. You only need to use them very sparingly to get the flavour.

Pistachios (fistíkia)

Salted and roasted in their shells, pistachios are the tastiest and most addictive of Greek nuts. They are, however, expensive. The best come from the island of Aegina just a few miles off the coast of Athens. If ever you are travelling by boat and make a stop there, the pistachio vendors swarm on board with their baskets under their arms to make as many sales as possible before the ship moves on. Take some home as a present if you want to bind your friends to you for life; they are on sale in the Duty Free Shop at Athens airport.

Stragália

Though they look like little round nuts, *stragália* are really salted, roasted chick-peas. Good, and among the least expensive nuts.

Walnuts (karídhia)

Walnuts are surprisingly inexpensive, given their scarcity and the labour of picking them. They are half the price of pistachios shelled, and very much cheaper unshelled. Like chestnuts they only grow in the mountains. If you should happen to travel there in October when they are being picked, you'll find practically everyone you meet has their hands stained black from the outer skins of the walnuts. They are used in stuffings and in a whole variety of cakes. Again, they make a good accompaniment to drinks, mixed with sultanas or raisins.

Walnuts

HERBS AND SPICES

Herbs in profusion grow wild all over the mountains and hillsides of Greece. If you arrive in Athens by air, their heady, almost intoxicating smell will be the first thing that greets you as you step from the plane onto the tarmac. Thyme is the predominating scent. And if you go for a walk almost anywhere in the Greek countryside away from cultivated ground, you can see it and scores of other wild herbs for yourself.

Described in ancient times, by Theophrastus in the fourth century B.C. and Dioscorides in the first century A.D., these herbs are still widely used in cooking and for medicinal purposes. No self-respecting Greek household would be without a stock of chamomile, for instance, for making tea to calm the nerves or mint to ease the stomach and cleanse the intestines. Like the French with their livers, the Greeks have a consuming preoccupation with the state of their *éndera* or intestines. Traditionally, these herbs would be gathered in the wild in due season, sun-dried and stored away for use. Though you can still buy them by the bunch in country markets, most are now sold dried and packaged in plastic boxes. They are usually labelled in Greek and English, though the translations are not always reliable. The same goes for spices too. Much cheaper than at home, light and easy to carry, they make good presents to take home, for yourself or friends.

Below are listed some of the commoner herbs and spices, along with their principal uses.

Allspice (bahári)

Although not of Greek origin, allspice is sometimes used in beef casseroles, in combination with nutmeg and cinnamon. The name *bahári* is simply the generic term for spices.

Aniseed (glikániso)

Aniseed puts the 'oo' in ouzo, so to speak; gives it that special flavour. But it is also used in making aniseed bread, pastries, and the beef stew with onions called *stifádho*. And mothers give it to their infants to ease digestion and wind and make them drowsy.

Basil (vasilikós)

Practically every courtyard and balcony in Greece has its tight round clump of basil growing in a pot. Crushed, the leaves give off a very strong minty smell, which is much appreciated and is said to keep flies away, which is one of the reasons why you often find basil placed close to a door or window. Workers often wear a sprig behind the ear too, perhaps for the same reason. In cooking, however, its only use is to flavour tomato sauces.

Bay (dháfni)

Bay leaves are used a lot in Greek cooking, especially in soups, stews and tomato sauces. They are sometimes also used with *souvlákia* (shish kebabs), threaded on the skewer between the meat chunks along with pieces of tomato, onion and peppers. The flavour is potent and they need to be used sparingly. Don't try to eat them!

Bay leaves boiled in water are a favourite hair rinse, especially for people with dark hair.

Capers (kápari)

Almost a weed, you see capers straggling

over walls and across patches of waste ground. But the flower is lovely, big, white and delicate with a mass of long purple stamens as fine as eyelashes. The bit you buy pickled is the unopened flower-bud. Dioscorides says they are for killing 'worms in the ears', whatever they are. Greeks today, however, use them more commonly for garnishing fish and mayonnaise and adding punch to potato and cabbage salads.

Chamomile (hamomíli)

Chamomile is one of the Greeks' great herbal panaceas. Boiled in water and drunk as a tea, preferably sweetened with wild honey, it is a cure for colds, chills, and stomach upsets. It sedates the nerves and, made into compresses, soothes tired eyes and irritated skin. Just the flower is used, dried. It comes out at Easter, a big, daisy-like flower, often growing in vast, thick carpets. You gather it by scooping up the flowerheads with an upward jerk of the hand, fingers splayed in a comb.

Cloves (garífalo)

Apart from their more obvious and mundane uses in sweets and pastry-making, stews and meat sauces, cloves are used by country people in the magical art of *ksemátiasma* – literally, un-eyeing someone, which means freeing them from the influence of the evil eye. Only certain people have this skill. If, for instance, your child falls unaccountably ill, you send for such a person, who will set light to the end of a clove, say some secret prayer, and the spell is lifted!

Cinnamon (kanéla)

Ground cinnamon is sprinkled on *rizógalo*, the Greek rice pudding, on fresh and baked apples and other desserts. It is also used in pastries, as the bark is in stews.

Dill (ánithos)

Fresh dill is available all year round at the greengrocer's, though it is also sold packaged. Principal uses are in salads, *dolmádhes* (stuffed vine leaves), *spanakópita* (spinach pie), *mayirítsa* (a special Easter soup eaten after the midnight service) and in various meat dishes.

Fennel (máratho)

You can find fresh fennel in the springtime, although, since the season is short, you are more likely to have to buy it packaged. It is used in pickling olives, in *spanakópita* and, sometimes, with grilled fish.

Lime flowers (tílio)

Lime flowers are boiled in water to make a tisane that calms the nerves and induces sleep. Sweetened with a teaspoon of honey, it is also good for sore throats and coughs.

Marjoram (mantzouràna)

In Greece marjoram is only used as a tisane, with the same properties as lime flowers.

Mint (dhiósmos)

Mint is often grown in pots in courtyards and on balconies, though you find it in the wild too. It is frequently used in combination with parsley and oregano in meat and vegetable dishes such as *keftédhes* (meat-balls), *biftékia* (hamburgers), stuffed courgettes, tomatoes and peppers. It can also be substituted for nutmeg in *tirópita* (cheese pie) and *kolokithópita* (courgette pie). Boiled in water it is good for stomach upsets and for combatting cholesterol.

Mountain tea (tsái tou vounóu)

Although the Greek name simply means

mountain tea, the plant it is made from is a woolly-leaved, yellow-flowered member of the mint family that only grows 1,500m to 1,800m (5,000ft to 6,000ft) up in the mountains. Shepherds and mountain villagers gather it when it is in flower in July and dry it. You can buy bunches of it in the markets or get it packaged in boxes at the grocer's. It is very cheap and very good. Like other tisanes you simply boil a few sprigs of it in water and sweeten it with honey.

Nutmeg (moshokáridho)

Nutmeg goes into cheese and chicken pies, pastries, stews and the white sauce that is used with *pastítsio*, *moussakás* and stuffed vegetables.

Oregano (rígani)

Probably the most widely used of all Greek herbs, it grows all over the place in scrubby ground, though it is mostly sold packaged. It is used in salads and stews, with chicken and grilled fish and various other charcoal grills – it goes particularly well with *païdhákia* and *souvlákia*. *Féta* cheese is often served with a pinch of oregano; so is bread grilled with olive oil.

Parsley (maïdanó)

You can buy fresh parsley all year round. One of the most widely used herbs, it goes well with salads, casseroled vegetables, boiled and baked fish, meatballs and many pulses. It is also used as a garnish.

Rocket (róka)

Sold fresh all through the winter months, *róka* has a strong peppery taste that adds an interesting piquancy to salads.

Rosemary (dhendrolívano)

Available all year round, the culinary use of rosemary in Greek cuisine is restricted to tomato sauces. But traditionally it also had other quite different uses, as a rinse for dark clothes and as a tisane for the stomach and insides generally.

Sage (faskómilo)

Another herb which is only used as a tisane in Greece, again for settling the stomach.

Savory (thróumbi)

A mountain herb used in the pickling of olives.

Thyme (thimári)

Its powerful scent literally assails the nostrils when you go walking on the scrubby hillsides. Bees love it and the honey it makes is the most expensive and most highly esteemed. Its only real culinary use is in making chicken stuffings — and pickling olives.

HONEY

Greek honey (*méli*) is excellent, though the very small and local scale of production makes it expensive. *Attiki* is about the best known commercial brand, named for the district round Athens, whose honey has been highly esteemed since ancient times. *Thimarísio*, the honey made by bees that feed on the flowers of wild thyme, is the most appreciated. Like all Greek honey, it is always runny and has a strong aromatic flavour. Homemade honey can often be bought in the country, so keep an eye out for it wherever you are staying.

Greeks eat honey with butter and bread for breakfast, put it in yoghurt and use copious amounts of it in making *baklavás*, *kataífi* and all those other mouth-watering sticky cakes (see page 133). It is a healthy and tasty substitute for sugar as a sweetener with the various tisanes (*see* Herbs and Spices) and, for that matter, with common or garden tea. A teaspoon of it boiled in water does wonders for sore throats, colds, headaches and stomach upsets. Women also use it as a face mask to purify and cleanse their skin.

OLIVES

Olives (*eliés*) have been a staple food of the Greek people for centuries. Along with bread, cheese and tomatoes they constituted the principal meal of most country people. Still today a peasant going out to work in the fields, or a shepherd to follow his flock in the mountains, takes a handful of olives, a piece of cheese and a couple of stone-hard rusks known as *paximádhia* wrapped in a cloth in his knapsack as all his food for the day. Of course, generally, everyone is far more prosperous nowadays and eats much more substantially than this, but olives are still considered an integral part of the diet. Apart from being simply nibbled as snacks, they are used in salads, as *mezédhes*, and almost invariably as an accompaniment to the pulses — lentils in particular. They are perhaps a bit of an acquired taste, but one you won't regret acquiring.

You can't really go anywhere in Greece without being aware of the olive. There are literally millions of trees, their gnarled, twisted trunks — often several hundred years old — as much a part of the landscape as the rocks that surround them. They were and still are one of the major props of the rural economy. They are slow growers and take many years to bear fruit, which is why in classical times, when wars were fought with battles hardly longer than a soccer match in duration and with scarcely more participants, the most ungentlemanly act you could perpetrate against your enemy was to chop his olive trees down.

Olives ripen in the autumn. But never make the mistake of trying to eat one straight from the tree. They hardly look appetising and the taste is revolting. All olives, even the ones you buy green, have to be cured before they become edible.

You buy them by the weight. Most common are the black ones, of which there are three main types. Those from the region of Kalamata in the south of the Peloponnese are considered the best. Large, smooth-skinned, sometimes pinkish, oval and slightly pointed, meaty and juicy — they are usually called *eliés kalamón* or *kalamátas*. The canned olives you buy at home — and in Greece — are mostly of this type.

Eliés Amfíssis, from the largest olive plantations in the country, near the town of Amfissa close to Delphi, are also highly regarded. Mauvish-black in colour, bigger and rounder than Kalamata olives, they are just as juicy and even meatier, but not quite as sweet. The commonest of all, the ones you are most likely to find at the smallest and remotest *bakáliko* or grocer's shop, are the little black wrinkled fellows known as *thróumba*, slightly salty and bitter in taste. They are the cheapest too.

You can also find green olives. Known as *tsakistés*, they too are rather salty and bitter. They are picked unripe from the tree, crushed – whence the name – and cured, sometimes with fennel. The canned version are usually stuffed with carrot, almonds or pickled cucumber, and served as *mezédhes* with an aperitif or used to garnish dishes.

Instinct always seems to prompt you to keep olives in the fridge, but it is not actually very good for them. It dries them out. Much better to put them in a bowl with a little olive oil and cover them just to keep the flies away.

OLIVE OIL AND COOKING FATS

In Greece practically every aspect of the preparation of food involves the liberal use of olive oil. It is used in frying, in meat, poultry and vegetable dishes, even in pastry-making and cakes. While traditionally all cooking was done with olive oil, you can find a variety of vegetable oils in Greece nowadays. The Greek cook, however, is still scornful of them, using them only for frying and even so only occasionally.

The unaccustomed non-Greek stomach often finds this liberal application of the oil bottle a bit too much of a good thing at first. Of course, if you are eating out, it is difficult to regulate the amount of oil in the food, and it is also true that tavernas frequently economise by overusing the same oil and by not buying the best quality in the first place. But if you're cooking for yourself, then you can easily make sure you get the best and regulate the quantity you use, so you get acclimatised slowly. You will soon find that, far from considering the food greasy, you come to enjoy the very nourishing qualities of good oil.

If you are not certain about your feelings on the subject of olive oil, then you'd be wise to go easy on the vegetable dishes known as *ladherá* – literally, oilies!

An unexpected and tasty use of oil is in making toast. Just brown a good thick slice of oil-brushed Greek bread under the grill and sprinkle a little oregano on it. Tavernas often serve bread grilled in this way in winter. *Féta* cheese is also often served with a dollop of oil and pinch of oregano.

Though the strict term for olive oil is *eleóladho*, it is usually called simply *ládhi* – oil. Crete, the island of Mytilene (the ancient Lesbos) and the Peloponnese are the chief producers. Cretan and Mytilenean oil is good, but light. The richer Peloponnesian oil is considered the best. The new oil is produced every autumn when the olives are harvested. There is no snobbery connected with vintage, so you don't have to worry about that! The pure olive oil is of first rate quality and much cheaper than at home, so it is well worth taking full advantage of it when cooking in Greece. It is sold in plastic bottles – the larger quantities in cans. If you are thinking of taking some home with you – all expatriate Greeks do – make sure it is a can, not a plastic bottle, otherwise you'll end up with impregnated hand luggage or a large bill for carpet-cleaning from the airline.

If you really don't want to use olive oil for all purposes like the Greeks, there are a variety of vegetable oils to choose from: sunflower oil, sesame oil, corn oil and various seed oils. The three most prominent brands of olive and vegetable oils and related products are Elais, Minerva and Xenia. Cooking fats are sold in plastic containers. Elais actually make one derived from olive oil.

7

LOCAL WINES, SPIRITS, BEERS & SOFT DRINKS

Vines like well-drained, sloping, chalky ground, plenty of sunshine and not much water – a bill that Greece fits admirably. Vineyards cover the landscape from the northern mountains to the remotest island. Wine has been produced here at least since the Bronze Age. Greeks drink it with every meal, though there is very little drunkenness, and even children are encouraged to take a dram.

A lot of wine is produced but on a small scale and in a fragmented manner, many peasants just producing enough for their own domestic consumption. Methods of course are primitive. The grapes are picked by hand, from August on, and pressed by foot as often as not in a farmer's own *patitíri.*

Although Greek wines have been exported for many years, one of the chief complaints against them has been their lack of consistency in quality and taste, partly, obviously, due to the prevailing methods of production. In recent years, however, great advances have been made and there are now a number of wines on the market which compare favourably with their Continental competitors.

WINES

Retsina

The best known of all Greek wines, retsina is the traditional drink of the people, rural and urban. Strictly speaking, retsina refers only to the white resinated wine. Its rosé counterpart is called *kokinéli.* Both are made in exactly the same way as other table wines. Their highly individual taste derives from the addition of a few pieces of special pine resin to the must during fermentation. They are removed later with the lees.

There are a great many local varieties of retsina, and tavernas often have their own, which they draw in orange tin jugs from vast wooden barrels ranged round the walls. It is a uniquely Greek product, made predominantly in Evia, the Peloponnese and central Greece.

Both the red and white versions are dry, rather rough wines with a most unusual aromatic flavour, not, admittedly, to the taste of all palates. The unappreciative compare it to camphorated oil. But it is a taste that can be acquired, even by outsiders, and once you have acquired it you will want to indulge it. It probably goes best with spicy traditional dishes. Most people recommend serving it chilled, and that certainly takes some of the edge off the taste. But if you become a real enthusiast you will enjoy drinking it at room temperature. It is definitely most interesting when taken from the barrel – *híma* or *varelísio*. If you have to settle for a bottled make, Kourtaki, Cambas and Boutari are the best to go for.

Other wines

With the exception of retsina, which belongs in a category by itself, Greek wines are marketed in three categories: those with an 'own label'; those with an Appellation of Origin; and country wines.

'Own label' wines are marketed under labels chosen by various commercial wine firms, and are often a blend of wines from different regions. Some of the best, and better known, Greek wines belong to this category.

Wines with an Appellation of Origin are wines from a specific well-defined area, marketed under a registered place name. Such wines have to comply with internationally established wine standards. They must originate from the specific vine-growing area designated by their registered place name. The vines that produce them must be grown on privileged soil and must belong to a selected variety cultivated according to approved and established techniques. And the wine must be made according to the traditional methods of the region and matured under conditions that improve its quality. The Appellation of Origin label guarantees a quality product that conforms to recognised standards. Many of the established commercial firms also produce wines with a registered place name. All these wines have the words 'appellation of origin' printed under their place name, so check for that when looking for a quality wine from a particular region.

Lastly, there are the country wines. These are produced all over the country, often by individual vine-growers, small co-operatives or tavernas. Inevitably the quality is very variable.

Listed below, by category, are some of the better known and better quality Greek wines.

Wines with an Appellation of Origin

Mantinia From the Peloponnese, which accounts for a large share of Greek wine output, *Mantinia*, produced by the vineyards round the ancient site of Mantinea, is a good dry, light, white wine with a mildly aromatic bouquet.

Nemea A dry full-bodied red, known locally as the 'Blood of Hercules', Nemea is grown just south of Corinth in the foothills of the mountains.

Patras A little further west, the vineyards behind the town of Patras produce a rich, sweet red wine, almost the colour of port, known as *The Mavrodaphne of Patras*. Too sweet to be drunk with a meal, it is best treated as a dessert wine. The same region also produces the light white *Patras* and the sweet amber-coloured liqueur wine *The Muscat of Patras*, made from white muscat grapes and also best drunk as an aperitif or dessert wine.

Rhodos A lot of the best wine is produced in the islands. *Rhodos* is a dry white from the island of Rhodes.

Santorini This sweet white liqueur wine is grown on the volcanic soil of the island of Thira. It is very strong, with a natural alcohol content of 17 per cent.

Samos Another well-known sweet after-dinner wine.

The Robola of Cephalonia A light dry white, usually served chilled as a table wine.

Cretan wines Crete also produces a variety of good liqueur wines, four of which are entitled to an Appellation of Origin. *Sitia*, *Daphnes*, *Archanes* and *Peza* are all full-bodied reds with a fruity bouquet, a bit on the heavy side, but good as after-dinner wines.

Naoussa Best of all the Greek Appellation of Origin wines is *Naoussa*, produced in the vineyards of western Macedonia in the north of the country, where the colder, damper climatic conditions make this wine closer in nature to the wines of northern Europe. It is a clean, light, dry red that can easily hold its own in the company of many French and Italian wines.

Zitsa Another northern wine with a famous name, though not in the same class as *Naoussa*, is the white *Zitsa* from a region close to the Albanian frontier, made famous by Byron's rather exaggerated account of a visit in the early-nineteenth century.

'Own label' wines

Achaia Clauss, Boutari, Cambas, Carras and Kourtakis are the five best known wine-making establishments that dominate the Greek wine market. In addition to Appellation of Origin wines, they also market wines under their own labels, some of which are among the most popular and best produced in Greece. Among these are: *Blanc de Blancs, Demestica, Lac des Roches, Cambas Blanc, Rotonda, Côtes de Meliton* and *Hymettus.*

Country wines

While they may lack the more refined taste of wines produced under more systematically controlled conditions, many country wines are very good. In fact, in our opinion, they very often have more character than the commercially bottled wines that have largely displaced them as the standard taverna drink in recent years. They are certainly more wholesome and free of any chemical stabilisers and preservatives. They are much cheaper too, so it is always worth asking for them.

Some of the better known country wines are the dark red wines of the island of Paros, the *Verdea* of the island of Zakinthos (Zante), the white wines of Evia, and the wines of the Halkidhiki peninsula and Mount Athos.

SPIRITS

Ouzo must be *the* distinctively Greek drink, a strong aniseed-flavoured aperitif, clear when taken neat, but turning a milky white when diluted with water, which is the way it is normally drunk. In summertime, in particular, it is the Greeks' favourite pre-dinner drink, taken on the veranda or at the local *kafenío* in the last light of the day. At the *kafenío* it was traditionally served with a small plate of *mezédhes* (see page 89), which were on the house, but now you invariably have to order – and pay for – any *mezédhes.*

Like wine buffs, ouzo buffs argue endlessly and arcanely about the merits of various types of ouzo. The two most celebrated kinds come from the island of Lesbos (or, as it is now called in Greek, Mytilene) and the little town of Tirnavos west of Mount Olympus. The Mytilene ouzo goes under the name of Barbayiannis, the chief export merchant. Other makes are produced by Votrys, Boutari and Cambas, but the most popular brands of all are No 12 and Sans Rival.

Brandy is another cheap and palatable spirit produced locally, by Votrys, Cambas and Metaxas among others. Metaxas is the most widely known, but all distillers produce three categories: three, five and seven star. None of these brandies – all referred to as *koniák*, in Greek – has the class of the French equivalent, so there is no real point in buying anything more expensive than the three-star. It tastes much more obviously of ripe grapes than the French brandy – a distinctly perfumed taste. It takes dilution with water well, and since it is cheap you don't feel you are committing sacrilege.

More distinctively Greek are the highly alcoholic schnapps-like *rakí*, *tsikoudhiá* and *tsípouro*, only the first of which is marketed bottled. It is also the lightest at a mere 46 per cent. The Cretan *tsikoudhiá* can reach 60 per cent, as can the similar *tsípouro*, which is made and drunk chiefly in the mountains of the mainland. Both are readily obtainable in *kafenía* in the right regions.

BEERS

There used to be a Greek beer, appropriately named Fix, but it is no more. It was brewed by the descendant of a Bavarian family that came to Greece in the mid-nineteenth century in the wake of modern Greece's first king, the Danish princeling Otho. Some 20 or 30 years ago their posters in village cafés of glamorous girls in somewhat provocative poses were the only warning signs that the Amercian-style commercialism that had already conquered Europe was about to overwhelm Greece as well. Greek-made beers today are all foreign brand lagers brewed under licence, like Amstel, Kaiser, Löwenbrau.

SOFT DRINKS

The same is true of the big-name soft drinks sold in Greece, like Coca-Cola, Seven-Up and their kind. There are, however, also a number of good indigenous products, in particular, orangeades, lemonades and squashes, notably those made by Ivi. And the recently marketed Amita pure fruit juices are more than a match for the imported brands both in price and quality.

8

SOME USEFUL TIPS ON SHOPPING IN GREECE

Shopping for food in Greece is not difficult, despite the language. You can always point and tasting is completely accepted, especially in the more old-fashioned shops, at least for items like olives and cheese. And Greeks are not at all shy about sign-language or using bits and pieces of any language they may know. Besides, many people nowadays speak English, although it is always courteous to try to say something Greek first, even if it is only *kaliméra* – good-day.

All weights and measures of course are metric. (See Weights and Measures for explanation of equivalents.) But it is not difficult to remember that half a kilo (*misó kiló*) is as near a pound as matters for most purposes, and quarter of a kilo (*éna tétarto*) is half a pound. One thing that makes Greek weights and measures simpler to master than some is the fact that they use kilos for liquids too. A litre is *éna kiló* (one kilo) and half a litre *misó kiló* – a pint, give or take a sip or two.

The most complicated and irksome aspect of shopping is mastering the veritable cat's cradle of opening hours. It is at its most complicated in Athens and the cities, where every type of shop has different hours. All, however, have three afternoons a week off, in addition to Sunday. Some close at siesta time every day and stay closed, while others reopen. All chemists are now closed all day Saturday, besides Sundays and Monday and Wednesday afternoons, though they post a list of the on-duty chemists on their doors. In Athens at least you can buy an English-language monthly called *The Athenian* which prints details of these complicated arrangements. In other towns, you'll just have to ask, for it won't be the same.

Luckily, in the country and in holiday resorts shopping hours are much more flexible. Apart from siesta time, which lasts about three hours, shops stay open from 08.00 to 20.00 (or even 21.00) six days a week, except, probably, for one early closing day in mid-week. Often they are open Sundays as well. This depends how far the local police are prepared to go in enforcing the law. But even then you will probably find your local shop will let you in the back door in an emergency.

We have listed the principal kinds of shops below with their names in Greek and an account of what you can expect to find in each. The distinctions are by no means absolute. A greengrocer, for instance, will often stock some groceries as well as things like cockroach poison, washing-up liquid and dustbin bags, especially if it is the main neighbourhood shop.

Don't try to bargain. That is only appropriate in shops selling obviously tourist goods. The prices, especially in small shops, will probably not be displayed, so it is just as well to start by asking the price of things you are interested in buying. A simple 'Please, how much does it cost?' and a pointing finger will do the trick. In Greek, you say, '*Parakaló, póso káni?*'

SHOPS

Bakery (*fóurnos*)

Greek bread (*psomí*) is excellent and is sold where it is baked. You can buy it fresh and hot from about 08.00 in the morning onwards. Since most bakers bake more than once, you can get fresh bread again in the evening when they reopen after siesta time – as you can also on Sunday morning.

The commonest kind of loaf is the lozenge-shaped half-kilo *fradzóla*, which comes in white (*áspro*) or brown, which is usually called *horiátiko* or village bread. The round flat *karvéli* loaves are excellent too. Occasionally you see loaves with attractive Byzantine designs printed on them, like old-fashioned butter stamps. These are called *prosforá* and are made for the church. In urban bakeries you can often get a sweet, cake-like bread called *tsouréki*, which although associated particularly with Easter is usually obtainable all year round. It is very good for breakfast. And very occasionally you see the most beautiful decorative wedding loaves, all covered with doves, foliage, ears of corns, bunches of grapes, whatever the baker's skill can produce.

Besides bread, bakeries also sell a wide range of sweets, cakes, biscuits and gâteaux, *tirópita* (cheese pies), soft drinks, milk and yoghurt. They also perform one very useful service.

If you have a dish you want to bake or roast, but do not have an oven, just take it along to the baker and he will put it in his oven for a small charge. No need to be shy about it: it is absolutely standard procedure; you see lots of village women do it.

Butcher (*hasápis*)

Butchers' shops vary from the clinical to the flyblown, with blood-clotted carcasses hanging nose down from hooks outside the door. The latter are mainly to be found in the more old-fashioned places. But you can take your pick according to what your stomach will stand.

Poultry is normally sold clean, with the giblets stuffed inside the carcase. If you ask, a butcher will always halve or quarter a bird for you. And they will cut meat any way you want, provided you can explain. Some Greeks tip their butcher on a regular basis to make sure they always get choice cuts. We have never found that to be necessary, and it almost certainly is not worth it for a short-term stay.

Paradoxically, the butcher's is also the place to go for frozen fish and vegetables as well as meat.

Cáva

A *cáva* is the Greek equivalent of the off-licence, except that it does not sell tobacco and you do not need a licence to sell alcohol. Open during normal shop hours, they sell wines, spirits, beer, soft drinks, nuts, raisins, crisps (called *tsips* in Greek) and so on. The more sophisticated ones sell a wide range of imported drinks too.

Fishmonger (*ihthiopolío*)

In most island fishing ports there will be a fish market (*psaragorá*) with several stalls together, rather than an isolated fishmonger. This is the place to get fresh fish, but go early, for the stalls open early and close around midday, by which time all the best buys have gone. If you don't like scaling and gutting, the fishmonger will do it for a small tip. Again, you need to go early for the best bargains.

To be sure of really fresh fish, you need to take your early morning dip on the beach where some fisherman keeps his boat.

Greengrocer (*manávis*)

The *manávis* is your regular fruit and veg merchant. In remote places, on the less frequented and semi-barren islands and up in the mountains, there won't be much of either fruit or veg. But distribution is much improved nowadays, and in most holiday places you can be sure of a good selection of produce.

Very often the *manávis* will stock basic groceries and household necessities as well. But always keep an eye on the weights and don't be surprised if he doesn't like you trying to choose your own fruit and veg.

Grocer (*bakális*)

Though strictly speaking a grocery, it is a moot point where a *bakáliko* – as the shop is called – turns into what the foreign visitor would term a supermarket. Most grocers now stock a whole range of household products, drinks, frozen food, dairy produce, toiletries in addition to the traditional rice, pasta, olives, cheese, salt cod and so forth.

Pandopolío

The word means a place which sells everything. And that is what it does: a combination of grocer and greengrocer. They have mainly been replaced by small supermarkets today.

Períptero

The *períptero* is a uniquely Greek institution. You can't walk for long in any Greek town or village without coming across one. Kiosk is the nearest word in English. Usually wooden and usually yellow, they are little square boxes with pitched roofs that stand on every street corner and along every pavement, selling everything under the sun. Newspapers, tobacco, toothpaste, postcards, contraceptives, pencils, stamps, ice-creams, chewing gum, sweets ... anything the *peripterás* thinks he can trade in from his stand. Many of them also have telephones for public use, which can save a long walk to the telephone company (OTE) building, at the end of which you are quite likely to find the place closed. Ask before trying to make an international call because sometimes the *peripterás* does not like it and his telephone is not up to it anyway.

Supermarket

The word is the same in Greek. It covers anything from the small corner shop to vast Athenian establishments stocked with all sorts of luxury imported goods. In general, supermarkets are groceries expanded to include household necessities. Very few do fruit and veg as well.

Zaharoplastío

In its function as a shop, a *zaharoplastío* (see page 89) sells pastries, sweets, cakes, biscuits, wine and spirits, soft drinks, and often milk and yoghurt. Those which also function as café-tearooms – the majority – are open every day, including Sundays, and stay open most of the day.

SERVICES

Banks (*trápeza*)

The only problem with banks is finding one open when you need it. They are closed weekends and afternoons from around 14.00.

Chemist (*farmakío*)

Chemists' shops are advertised by a green cross on a white ground outside. They stock a wide range of pharmaceutical products, first-aid necessities and toiletries. Again, the range depends on how busy and prosperous the local community is. You can ask chemists for advice on basic ailments and minor injuries. You would be wise to exercise a little caution in accepting some of their drug recommendations. There is a general tendency in Greek medicine to prescribe large doses of strong drugs, many of which can be sold over the counter by a chemist without your requiring a doctor's prescription.

OTE

This is the acronym of the Greek telephone company. They have offices in nearly every small town, where you can go to make your calls. Make sure you know the overseas dialling code in case you want to telephone home when you are in Greece. In big towns OTE is open for calls round the clock. In smaller places they close as early as 15.00.

Post Office (*tahidhromío*)

City Post Offices stay open until late. Small offices close around 15.00. All are closed at weekends. Any office will keep mail for you, if you have it addressed to Poste Restante; in order to collect it you will be asked to produce your passport. Letterboxes are few and far between and often look very neglected. It is safest to do your posting at the Post Office.

9

WHAT TO TAKE WITH YOU

Travel light is always a good general principle. You don't want to clutter your luggage with pots and pans and jars of jam. And holidaying in Greece nowadays you need hardly take anything with you. Tourism is well developed. In all the major destinations, like Crete, Corfu, Rhodes and Spetses, you will find supermarkets stocking a wide range of local and imported foods and household necessities. In fact, this is true throughout Greece except for the remotest places, for the Greeks themselves are much more prosperous than they used to be and now travel widely in their own country during the summer months. What is more, with the steady decline in the value of the drachma against other currencies, there is no longer any real saving in taking once expensive items like tea and coffee with you.

If you are renting rooms or a villa equipped for self-catering, you are obviously at the mercy of the tour company as far as the completeness of the equipment goes. If you find any major deficiencies, we suggest you bully the local representative first.

Here, however, are a few suggestions for small items that can make life easier. First priorities should be a good cork-screw/tin-opener that you know works and a couple of sharp kitchen knives that can be used also as carving and bread knives. A pair of tough all-purpose scissors that cut anything from chicken bones to wire would be useful too. And you won't regret taking a timer, cheese-grater – preferably flat for ease of packing – a small plastic measuring jug calibrated in grams and ounces and perhaps a measuring spoon as well, some plastic egg-cups (the Greeks don't use them) and a few pieces of tupperware.

Although they are readily obtainable in Greece, it is worth packing a few basics to tide you over the first night, if need be, like tea bags, a small tin of instant coffee and powdered milk, a few airline-style sachets of sugar, salt and pepper, a pack of plastic freezer bags and a roll of toilet paper. And don't miss your ration of duty-free alcohol. There is no point in worrying about wine, but spirits will be a good deal cheaper than in a Greek liquor store.

An item that we find invaluable, especially when you have children, is a cool-bag or two and a selection of ice-packs that you can activate in the fridge freezer compartment. (Cool food and drink make all the difference to beach picnics.) If you get the better quality ones with a cloth exterior, they are strong enough to use as carrier bags on the journey as well. A thermos, or similar, is also a useful addition.

As to the question of whether or not to take more substantial kitchen equipment, it depends on how much cooking you plan to be doing and for how many people. The most uncumbersome and practical mechanical aid is a small hand-held electric blender, which would certainly simplify some of the recipes in this book. A non-stick electric frying pan with lid would be very useful too if you were cooking a lot. But any electrical equipment you bring will need to have the plugs changed – though Greek voltage, at 220V, is the same as in Britain and some other countries. It would be no bad thing for this and other reasons to take a few basic tools with you. An electrical screwdriver, a small pair of pliers and a small adjustable spanner (for gas bottles, cooker jets and the inevitable things that get stuck) make a good minimum kit.

Camping gas is widely available in Greece. Although you cannot travel with the bottles on an aircraft, you might take the fittings with you if you have them. That would give you a useful and flexible reserve cooking facility.

An item you might consider buying once arrived in Greece is a small barbecue (*psistariá*). The basic kind, consisting of a tray on legs, is all you need. The cost is scarcely more than the price of a meal for one. As a further indication of the value of your own barbecue it is fair to say that the cost of one pork chop, eaten at a taverna, is about 75 per cent more than buying five yourself at the butcher's. Charcoal (*kárvouna*) is easy to come by, as Greeks do a lot of cooking on barbecues. A really good investment, we think.

Another thing you might get yourself, especially if you acquire a taste for Greek coffee, is a small alloy coffee pot called a *bríki* – very cheap, and something you can easily take home with you.

A word about medicines, toiletries and the like. Greek chemists stock a wide variety of products, of Greek and foreign origin, and you will have no trouble finding what you want, though the brand names may be different. Even so, it is a sensible precaution to take a basic first-aid kit; plasters (band-aids), aspirin, antiseptic cream, something to settle the stomach and cope with diarrhoea, something to soothe insect bites, jellyfish stings and sunburn. Before you leave home ask your local chemist to make up a suitable kit for you.

Mosquitoes are a problem in the summer. You'll need something in your room at night to keep them away. You can buy a small electrical device called a Vape-Nat in Greece, which activates a chemical tablet, as well as some slow-burning coils known as Moon Tigers. But you will also need something to protect yourself when you go out in the evening. The spray repellents are best; not only do they reach parts other creams don't, they don't make you all sticky!

It is worth arriving armed with a supply of suntan oil. It is expensive in Greece as elsewhere, although widely available. If you buy suntan oil locally, especially if you are systematic about your tanning and particular about using the right grade of protection at the right stage, you may find your entire strategy ruined because the grades you want have sold out.

One last suggestion: pack a small torch (flashlight). It always comes in handy for negotiating village lanes after dark or making your way to a midnight swim.

10

FOOD FOR BABIES, CHILDREN, AND THOSE ON SPECIAL DIETS

Relying as it does on such staples as pulses, fresh vegetables, fruit and fish, the traditional Greek diet is a healthy one and should be readily adaptable to meet most straightforward dietary requirements. There are, however, no health food shops in Greece outside Athens and while you can rely on chemists to supply any vitamin pills you may require, special dietary products may be harder to find. Sugar substitutes, sugar-free fruit juices, biscuits, jams, macaroni and other foods do exist, often of foreign manufacture, but you will not find them away from urban centres and tourist resorts. The same applies for rye bread, which most city bakeries make specially for diabetic regimes.

So, apart from taking the obvious precaution of asking your doctor's advice before you set off on foreign travels, you should be aware that specialised products will be unavailable anywhere off the beaten tourist track.

LOW FAT DIETS

The temptation to eat hot, fresh bread, sticky cakes and rich yoghurts is strong in Greece. But if you can control these urges, you can make a varied, tasty and colourful diet for yourself, using the marvellous vegetables and fruit that are available for most of the year. Fresh fish is obtainable anywhere close to the sea – and is much more plentiful off-season – and chicken is a good standby wherever you go. Low-fat milk and yoghurt are also available nowadays. Even eating out will not involve you in too many painful struggles with your conscience, for so much taverna food is grills and salads.

DIABETIC DIETS

You will already be aware of the do's and don'ts of your own particular diabetic regime, and as long as you are catering for yourself you will have no difficulty eating in an agreeable and balanced way. You will not, however, find a great many sugar-free products on the market outside Athens. Greek ready-made foods and drinks tend to have a high sugar content.

HIGH FIBRE DIETS

The predominant place of pulses, vegetables and fruit in the Greek diet makes following a high fibre regime a simple business. Nuts and dried fruits are also widely available. Traditional breakfast cereals and porridge oats can only be found in places frequented by tourists.

BABIES

As long as you stick to the beaten track, you will find most supermarkets and groceries carry Greek and imported baby-foods and disposable nappies (diapers). Every bakery in the land makes rusks (*paximádhia*), and you will find that condensed and powdered milk are also almost universally available.

OLDER CHILDREN

Despite their natural conservatism about eating unfamiliar foods, feeding children in Greece is not really a problem, even when eating out. You have no worries about making them sit still and behave themselves, for you are nearly always eating out of doors and most tavernas are full of Greek children playing tag between the tables and teasing the stray cats that loiter hopefully in the offing.

Your children may not like the oily dishes, but these are easily avoided. The grilled shish kebabs (*souvlákia*), chops (*brizóles*) and hamburgers (*biftékia*) and the fried but oil-free meat-balls (*keftédhes*) are always popular. Chicken is on practically every menu and chips are served with absolutely everything. Although restaurants do not normally serve ice-cream themselves, there is invariably a café or *períptero* not far away which does, and the kids can be dispatched to rummage in the freezer for the tub or cone of their choice. The restaurant will not mind in the least.

The freedom and security that children can enjoy in Greece will more than compensate for any inconvenience. The Greeks are very indulgent towards children and pay them a lot of attention. Crimes against children are practically unheard of and you can confidently leave the children to wander about on their own – within reason, of course.

11

EATING AND DRINKING OUT

Who knows which comes first, climate, temperament or culture? Whichever it is, the Greeks, like other southern peoples, live a lot of their lives outside their homes. They eat out, drink out, sit in cafés and talk, just put a chair in the street and watch the world go by. There are in consequence lots of places to go and a precise etiquette regulating where you go and what you eat or drink at different times of the day. And it's cheap, especially by comparison with other European countries. One person can have a good, filling meal with wine for less than the cost of a beer and sandwich in their own country.

The principal headings in this section are the different kinds of restaurant (taverna and *estiatório*), the *kafenío* or café (which is still a largely masculine domain) and the *zaharoplastío*, a sort of café-cum-patisserie, which is much more accessible to women and children. You will find a description of the Greek customs connected with each establishment and the kind of thing you can expect to do or buy there. We assume, as we have all through this book, that you want to do things the Greek way. There are, of course, lots of 'English pabs', 'brekfast' joints and other such establishments nowadays that try to make foreigners feel they have not left home.

RESTAURANTS

The quality of Greek restaurants varies enormously, and does not necessarily improve with the price or apparent chic of the surroundings. This is especially true of places frequented by tourists.

So the first rule of eating out should be to eat where the Greeks eat. And the Greeks eat late. They lunch as late as

15.00 and dine at 21.00 or 22.00 – even later in the summer. If you stick to your own stomach clock, you'll never ever see any Greeks eating!

If you want your eating to be even a half-way Greek experience, don't go to any restaurant that is serving dinner around 18.30 or 19.00. It can only be catering for tourists, as no self-respecting Greeks have recovered from their siestas at that hour. The restaurant is probably offering a restricted menu, vaguely international food, indifferent quality and inflated prices. Tourists are docile customers; they won't complain and are soon gone, so there is no fear of losing trade. Pulling a fast one, being smarter than the dumb foreigner is very much part of the Greek way of doing things, even if it is disguised with a smile and flattering words.

Another rule should be to avoid smart-looking places, if you are after quality and Greekness. You will only be paying for the linen tablecloth, the napkin folded in a stemmed wine glass and the bronze candelabra. If the menu is any different from the place with paper tablecloths and toothmugs for glasses, it will be in the addition of foreign or international dishes, which few Greek chefs have any experience of. This is not to say there are no extremely good high-class restaurants, but they are confined mainly to the Athens area. Greece does not have the tradition of sophisticated professional cooking found in France or Italy. In the islands and seaside places you are likely to find yourself in, the restaurants will often be run by people who were water-ski instructors or builders last year and have decided there is more money in feeding the tourists this year.

Don't be fooled by plastic and the appearance of modernity, nor by the very insistent 'Yes please. This way. Very nice Greek food' that you'll often hear from waiter-touts who loiter outside their premises to ensnare the passing foreigner. Often the simplest-looking places are the best. Some, for instance – usually *psistariés*, which specialise in roast kid and lamb (see page 87) – don't even give you a plate. They simply dump your order in a sheet of paper directly on the table top. The paper is fresh for each new customer, don't worry! But if you shied away from such a place because it looked too primitive, you'd be missing something good.

Greek cuisine is popular cooking, what everyone eats at home, rich and poor alike. And this is what Greek chefs do best. There is no tradition of eating foreign to eat well and none of the connotations of wealth and snobbery have ever been attached to eating out. It was just as much a poor man's practice, and this is reflected in the décor of the traditional

Greek restaurant. It is a simple, basic place with a stone floor, bare walls, wooden tables and chairs.

Perhaps for similar reasons, you should not expect elaborate manners from the waiters. But you can't get revenge by leaving no tip, as a service charge is always included in the bill. Furthermore you are expected to leave a little something for the 'boy' who plonked the knives and forks on the table and did not bring the water when you asked.

Greeks themselves are relatively big spenders. When they go out they like to make a splash. It is considered bad form to be careful with your money in public. So they tend to order a lot more than they can eat, almost as if it were a point of honour to be able to afford to waste food in a nonchalant manner. This practice creates certain problems if you are trying to be budget-conscious. For you will find waiters push you to order more than you want and even bring you things you did not order. However, don't hesitate to send them back. And be a bit careful about your bills too. Waiters seldom write anything down. They come at the end of the meal to examine the plates to see what you have had. Then the bill is invariably illegible, even if you read Greek. So the opportunities for slipping in a few drachmas here and a few drachmas there are quite considerable, especially in many of the more popular places which disdain such details as menus and published prices altogether.

If you ever eat with Greek friends, the end of the meal is invariably good entertainment, for it always ends in a theatrical quarrel over who is going to pay the bill. The Greeks are extremely generous and will fight vehemently for the privilege. So if you don't want to be paid for every time, you have to learn to outwit them, for instance, by sneaking off to the loo before the end of the meal and making a secret deal with the waiter.

As a general rule, the less a place is used to holidaymakers, foreign or Greek, the better you will be treated. This is not intended to put you off. Eating out is always enjoyable in Greece. You sit outside. The nights are warm. The atmosphere is relaxed. There is none of the stuffiness or reserve common in restaurants here.

Estiatória

There are two basic types of restaurant: the *estiatório* (*estiatória* is the plural form) and the taverna. The former is mainly an urban or at least small town institution. It is a place people go to for their midday rather than evening meal, and you are more likely to eat indoors.

What distinguishes the *estiatório* from the taverna is the food it serves. The *estiatório* specialises in the more complicated cooked dishes: *moussakás*, *pastítsio*, all the *ladherá* dishes, stews like *kokkinistó* and *stifádho*, *yemistá* (stuffed tomatoes and peppers), pasta, *soutzoukákia* (rice and meatballs), the oven-cooked meat and fish dishes, and so on. The cooking is done once, in the morning, and left to stand, which is why it is often lukewarm or even cold. This is something which does not bother Greeks at all. In fact, if you complain about your food being cold, the waiter is quite likely to react with total incomprehension. And it is true that it hardly seems to matter with many of these dishes if they are not served piping hot, especially in summertime. The *ladherá* and *yemistá*, for instance, actually seem to be enhanced by being allowed to cool off standing in their own juices.

Desserts really do not exist, although fruit is always available in season. Wine and beer is served; Greek coffee may be, although Greeks themselves do not normally drink coffee immediately after a meal.

Tavernas

Tavernas are much more common than *estiatória*. They range from the chic and fashionable to rough and ready cabins with a bamboo awning set up by the beach in summer. They are generally relaxed and informal, with most of their tables ranged out of doors on a street or quayside or in a garden.

The primitive ones have only a limited choice of menu, but the more established will offer some of the main *estiatório* dishes mentioned above as well as the standard taverna fare. This essentially means starters or *mezédhes* and *tis óras*, dishes of meat and fish fried or grilled to order.

Since the idea of courses is foreign to Greek cuisine, starters or appetizers, main dishes, and salads often arrive together or in reverse order. The best thing is to order a selection of starters and salads to share among you; that, after all, is what Greeks do. Waiters encourage you to take the *horiátiki* salad – the so-called Greek salad – because it is the most expensive. If you only want tomato or tomato and cucumber, ask for *domatosaláta* or *angourodomáta*. *Maróuli* (lettuce) and *láhano* (cabbage) are the winter salads.

The most interesting starters are *tzatzíki* (yoghurt, garlic and cucumber dip), *melitzanosaláta* (eggplant dip), courgettes or eggplant fried in batter (*kolokithákia tiganitá*, *melitzánes tiganités*), *yígandes* (butter beans in vinaigrette sauce), small cheese and spinach pies (*tiropitákia, spanakópites*), *saganáki* (fried cheese), octopus (*ohtapódhi*) and *mavromátika* (black-eyed beans).

Of meats, *souvláki* (shish kebab) and *brizóles* (chops) are reliable choices. In both cases, pork (*hirinó*) is usually better than veal (*mosharísio*). The best *souvláki* is lamb (*arnísio*), but it is not often available. The small lamb cutlets called *païdhákia* are very tasty, as is roast lamb (*arní psitó*) and roast kid (*katsíki*) when obtainable. *Keftédhes* (meat-balls), *biftékia* (sort of hamburger) and the spicy sausages called *loukánika* are cheap and good, especially if you don't like olive oil.

Seaside tavernas of course also offer fish. *Kalamarákia* (fried baby squid) are a summer staple. The choicer fish, however, are expensive: *barbóunia* (red mullet), *lithrínia* (pandora), *fangrí* (sea bream) and so on. The price is quoted by the kilo, and the standard procedure is to go to the fridge and choose your own. Again, you have to resist the waiter's efforts to make you buy more than you need. The cheapest widely available fish are *gópes* (bogue) and *marídhes* (tiny picarel, eaten whole, head and all). The Greeks tend to eat the latter only as a *mezés*, though a whole plateful is pretty filling.

As with *estiatória*, desserts are more or less non-existent. Watermelons, melons and grapes are the standard summer fruit. Tavernas will offer you a better choice of wines. Cambas and Boutari *Rotonda* and *Lac des Roches* are good among the cheaper bottled ones. If you want something better, the Boutari *Naoussa* is hard to beat. Otherwise, go for the local wines. Retsina is invariably better straight from the barrel. Not as many tavernas keep it as used to, but always ask whether they have wine *apó to varéli* or *híma* – both mean, in effect, 'from the barrel'.

Some tavernas specialise. *Psarotavérnes*, for instance, specialise in fish, *psistariés* in spit-roasted lamb and goat or *kokorétsi* (grilled offal). A few specialise in game (*kinígi*): wild boar, hare – quail in the autumn, when the migrating flocks fly over Greece on their way south. In the mountains of the north where there are rivers, trout, pike and freshwater crayfish are caught and you will find them in the local eating places.

Most eating places today print their menus in English as well as Greek. Not that that is always a help. *Mysterious, file mignone mad, slice, fiddlesticks with garlic sauce, small boot stuffed eggplant* are just a sample of the dishes we have not been able to trace in any nation's cookery books. But if you do have any difficulty understanding what is on offer, head straight for the kitchen and point. It is the accepted procedure.

SNACKS

The commonest Greek snacks are *tirópita* and *koulóuri*. *Tirópita* is a flaky pastry pie filled with cheese – bigger than the kind served in restaurants as a *mezés*. There is nearly always a supply of them warming on a hot plate on the counter of the bakery in the morning. Sometimes even *períptera*, the corner kiosks, sell them, as do the little hole-in-the-wall stalls.

A *koulóuri* is a crispy-baked, ring-shaped kind of bread covered with caraway seeds. You find them at the baker's or sold on the streets of towns. In Athens you still see boys carrying piles of them balanced on a board on their heads.

A favourite snack with bus and ferry passengers are small *souvlákia* (shish kebabs) on a wooden skewer. They are usually sold at stalls near long-distance bus stops and ferry embarkation points. Sometimes they are served with a piece of pitta bread filled with *tzatzíki*, peppers, tomatoes and onions. The town of Livadhia on the way to Delphi is particularly well known for its *souvlákia*, and the little village of Mili as you go south from Argos to Sparta in the Peloponnese.

A rather similar snack is the *yíro*, again with pitta bread, but instead of the *souvláki* you have pieces of meat sliced from a sort of compacted column of meat rotated on a vertical spit.

Also common nowadays are a variety of sandwich bars, fast food establishments and pizza places. If you see '*tost*' advertised, that means toasted sandwiches.

Kafenía

The *kafenío* is the traditional Greek coffee-shop or café. Although its main business is Greek coffee, it also serves spirits such as ouzo and brandy, beer, tea (either herbal mountain tea or European, i.e. British-style, tea), soft drinks, *glikó tou koutalióu* (sticky, syrupy preserves of grape or fig, orange or cherry) and the old-fashioned *ipovríhio*, which is a piece of mastic submerged in a glass of water like a submarine, which is what *ipovríhio* means in Greek.

Another very agreeable summer drink you can get in the more modern cafés is *kafé frapé*, a sort of iced instant coffee – a uniquely Greek drink despite its French-sounding name. (To see how to make this, and ordinary Greek or Turkish coffee, see page 136).

Like tavernas, *kafenía* range from the plastic and sophisticated – which serve fewer of the traditional Greek drinks and more imported Western-style drinks, milk-shakes and so on – to the old-fashioned spit-on-the-floor variety, with marble-topped or brightly painted metal tables and wooden chairs with straw seats. An important institution anywhere in Greece, they are the central pivot of life in the country villages. The men go there to discuss business, talk politics, play cards, and generally organise life the way they want it without reference to their womenfolk. In fact, you get the impression that many men spend most of their waking hours there. And women are definitely not welcome. In remote places, even male strangers are eyed with suspicion.

This is no longer true of the towns and holiday resorts. But there too, if you look carefully, you will find there is at least one café that the local men have kept intact for themselves.

Some *kafenía* close at siesta time, but many remain open from early in the morning until late at night. On the whole, the bigger the trade, the longer they stay open. But the chief socialising time is from around 18.00 immediately after the siesta. This is the time to take your pre-dinner ouzo, as the sun begins to sink and the heat cools – it gets dark much earlier in summertime than in northern climes, around 21.00 at the latest. You will be served two glasses, one with the ouzo, and one full of water, to be tipped into your ouzo until it turns a milky white. You can drink it neat, but its strong, burning taste is hardly refreshing if you do.

Until not long ago, every ouzo you ordered was automatically accompanied by a small plate of *mezédhes*, on the house: bits of cheese, cucumber, tomato, a few olives, sometimes octopus or even a couple of small fish. The Greeks rightly believe that alcohol on an empty stomach is not a good thing. By the time you had downed three or four ouzos you had had a free meal. But those days, alas, are gone. If you want *mezédhes* now, you have to ask for them, and pay. It is still very cheap by most European standards.

Though their number seems to be diminishing rapidly, there is a kind of drinking establishment which specialises in ouzo and *mezédhes*, called an *ouzerí*. These are well worth trying for the marvellous variety of *mezédhes* they serve.

Zaharoplastía

The *zaharoplastío* is best defined by what it sells. Its particular speciality is sweets, cakes and biscuits of various kinds, ranging from French-style confections of cream and chocolate to honey-dripping Greco-Turkish sweets like *baklavás* and elaborate gâteaux. These can either be consumed on the premises or bought by the kilo to take away. If you buy to take away, you will be asked if it is for a present (*dhóro*), for Greeks often give sweets and cakes as presents on name-days and when they go visiting. If you say yes, you will get a fancy wrapping with satin bows and ribbons.

There is an enormous variety of *zaharoplastío* goodies. Here, for the sweet-toothed, is a brief description of a few of the commonest and most typically Greek. The best known of all is probably *baklavás* (see page 133). It is made of buttered layers of very thin leaf-like pastry called *fílo*, stuffed with chopped walnuts and drenched in honey. It is sold in squares, diamonds and small rolls.

Another desperately fattening and irresistible confection is *galaktobóureko*, a sort of pie, again made of *fílo*, and filled with a soft, melting mixture of milk, semolina and eggs, the whole soaked in a syrup of sugar and lemon juice. Then there is *kataífi*, which looks like sausage rolls made of shredded wheat, filled with almonds and walnuts, and – you've guessed it – drenched in honey. A great children's favourite are *dhíples*: light, crispy pastry bows covered with honey syrup and sprinkled with finely chopped nuts.

If you still insist you have the strength of will to resist these temptations, we dare you to try fresh, hot *loukoumádhes* (see page 135). They are little balls of frothy, light batter fried in olive oil, dusted with cinnamon and dipped in a syrup of sugar and honey. They are particularly good for breakfast! Less gooey but nearly as addictive are the round almond-cakes known as *kourabiédhes*, dredged with icing sugar and presented in great pyramid-like mounds on the *zaharoplastío* counter. To say nothing of the many others …

In general, the *zaharoplastío* is a more sophisticated place than the *kafenío*. They serve Continental-type breakfasts of *méli me voútiro* (honey with butter) or jam and fresh bread. All jam, incidentally, is called *marmeládha* in Greek. If you want what we normally call marmalade, you must ask for *marmeládha portokáli* (orange jam). You are also more likely to find proper tea and different kinds of coffee at a *zaharoplastío*. *Neskafé* has become the general Greek word for all instant coffee, regardless of brand. Other things you can commonly buy are bottles of wine and spirits to take away, yoghurts and ice-creams.

If you have conceived an uncontrollable passion for Greek sweet things, you will enjoy a visit to perhaps the most famous of all *zaharoplastía*, Varsos, in the smart northern Athenian suburb of Kifissia. There you can buy all manner of pastries, gâteaux, ice-creams, home-made jams and yoghurt by the weight, the likes of which you have never tasted before.

12

SOME IDEAS FOR MENUS

As we have remarked elsewhere in this book, the idea of a formal succession of courses is really alien to Greek eating habits. The menus that follow here have been composed simply to give an idea of what dishes combine well together. You could of course combine them in any way you think fit. And any of these menus can easily be expanded by the addition of extra starters.

Picnics are the best midday meal in summertime, especially if you want to stay by the sea all day. We have already recommended a cool-bag, but even with one it is a mistake to take things like butter out in the midday heat. The best picnic ingredients are bread, cheese, olives, tomatoes, cucumber and fruit.

For good, simple evening meals there is nothing to beat the barbecue. With charcoal-grilled meat or fish as the main course, all you need to prepare extra is a couple of starters and salads, with fruit to follow.

MENUS

Menu 1

Shish kebab (*souvlákia*)
French fries or
Pilaf with tomato sauce (*piláfi me sáltsa domátas*)
Salad and cheese
Fruit

Menu 2

Spinach with rice (*spanakórizo*)
Fried picarel (*marídhes tiganités*)
Salad
Fruit

Menu 3

Spinach pie (*spanakópita*)
Roast chicken (*kotópoulo sto fóurno*)
Tomato salad (*domatosaláta*)
Fruit

Menu 4

Beetroot salad (*padzária saláta*)
Fried cod (*bakaliáros tiganitós*)
Garlic sauce (*skordhaliá*)
Fruit

Menu 5

Fish roe dip (*taramosaláta*)
Olives
Haricot bean soup (*fasoládha*)
Green salad
Fruit

Menu 6

Veal casserole (*moshári stifádho*) or
Veal with tomato sauce (*moshári kokinisto*)
Potato purée or pilaf rice
Salad
Crème caramel (*kréma karamelé*)

Menu 7

Macaroni, baked with minced meat (*pastítsio*)
Green salad
Cheese
Fruit

Menu 8

Okra in oil (*bámies ladherés*)
Fish roe dip (*taramosaláta*)
Black olives
Fruit

Menu 9

Mussels with pilaf rice (*mídhia me piláfi*)
Salad
Olives
Fruit

Menu 10

Tinned sardines in oil
Féta cheese
Black olives
Lentil soup (*fakés sóupa*)
Green salad
Fruit

Menu 11

Roast lamb with potatoes (*arní me patátes*)
Salad and cheese
Fruit

Menu 12

Courgette pie (*kolokithópita*)
Tomato and cucumber salad (*angourodomáta saláta*)
Yoghurt and walnut dessert (*yiaóurti me méli ke karídhia*)

Menu 13

Stuffed tomatoes and peppers (*domátes ke piperiés yemistés*
Cheese
Fruit

Menu 14

Wild greens (*hórta*)
Grilled fish (*psári sti skára*)
Fruit

Menu 15

Yellow lentils (*fáva*)
Fried fish
Salad
Cheese
Fruit

Menu 16

Chicken with okra
(*kotópoulo me bámies*)
Cheese
Rice pudding (*rizógalo*)

Menu 17

Baked sardines (*sardhéles sto fóurno*)
Potato salad (*patatosaláta*)
Cheese
Fruit

Menu 18

Octopus in wine sauce
(*ohtapódhi krasáto*)
Pilaf rice
Green salad
Fruit

Menu 19

Minced meat and rice-balls
(*yiourvarlákia me sáltsa domátas*)
Pilaf rice
Salad and cheese
Fruit

13

RECIPES

The 93 recipes in this section have been chosen principally for their Greekness and their interest. As it happens, most of them are very straightforward, requiring no unusual ingredients or sophisticated mechanical aids. A small electric blender would be helpful, but is far from indispensable. Otherwise, a frying pan, a couple of saucepans with lids and a baking dish will see you through.

In Greece, if you have the use of a proper cooker, it will certainly be electric. If you only have rings, you'll be using bottled gas. Greek cooker ovens are not very responsive to their controls. You generally have to be content with hot and not so hot, regardless of the temperature calibrated on the control knobs. When we say moderate ovens we mean around 180 degrees Centrigrade or 350 degrees Fahrenheit. When we say hot, we mean around 200 degrees Centigrade or 400 Fahrenheit. But you will have to get acquainted with your machine before you can regulate its behaviour.

If you have no oven at all, all is not lost. You simply do what Greek cooks have done for generations: you get your food oven-ready in a *tapsí* – a round Greek baking dish – and, as we said earlier, take it along to your local baker, who for a small charge will cook it in his bread ovens.

Quantities are expressed in kilos and grams with a rough equivalent in pounds; (see Weights and Measures for equivalents.) A cup means a regular teacup.

With the exception of the starters, which are customarily shared in Greece, the recipes in this section are designed for four people.

SAUCES AND DRESSINGS

The number of sauces used in traditional Greek cooking is

relatively limited. They are used mainly in the preparation of or as an accompaniment to fish, meat, vegetable and pasta dishes. The principal ingredients are tomatoes, onions, garlic and olive oil, used in various guises, the consistency and flavour varying to suit the requirements of particular dishes.

Salad dressings are essentially two: *ládhi ke lemóni* (olive oil and lemon juice) and *ladhóxidho* (olive oil and vinegar). Another variation of the *ládhi ke lemóni* dressing is the *ladholémono* sauce used with fish, which is made with the addition of a little parsley.

White sauce, known in Greece as *besamél* – a hellenisation of the French *béchamel* – though not of Greek origin, is widely used with pies, pasta and vegetable dishes.

Garlic sauce (*skordhaliá*)

If you have a taste for garlic you will enjoy this piquant sauce, which is most commonly served with fried cod and fried aubergines and courgettes.

6-8 cloves garlic
3-4 slices stale bread or 1 kg (2 lb) potatoes
2 cups olive oil
salt
4 tablespoons vinegar or the juice of 1 lemon
parsley and black olives (optional)

If you are using potatoes, they should be boiled for one hour in salted water. When they have cooled, peel and cut them into small pieces. Place the pieces in a blender together with the garlic, crushed or finely sliced. Add salt and vinegar (or lemon juice) and blend. Add the olive oil a little at a time, until all the ingredients have been thoroughly absorbed and the sauce is a nice smooth texture. It should not be runny. The ideal consistency is such that when a spoonful is placed on a plate it should hardly spread. Garnish with chopped parsley and olives.

If you are using bread instead of potatoes, first remove the crusts and soak the bread in water for about five minutes. Then squeeze dry and proceed in the same manner as for potatoes. It is easier to make *skordhaliá* with bread, although potatoes give the sauce more body and taste.

The sharpness of the sauce can be varied according to the amount of garlic used. After you have tried it a couple of times, you will know how much garlic suits your taste. If the sauce has come out too thick, you can loosen it by the addition of 1-2 tablespoons of water.

Olive oil and lemon dressing (*ládhi ke lemóni*)

Widely used with both raw and cooked salads, this dressing goes particularly well with Savoy cabbage, cauliflower and *hórta*.

3 tablespoons olive oil
1 tablespoon lemon juice
salt and pepper

Mix the oil and lemon juice together, season, and pour over salad.

Olive oil and lemon sauce (*ladholémono*)

Ladholémono is served with boiled and grilled fish and with lobster.

6 tablespoons olive oil
2 tablespoons lemon juice
salt and pepper
1 tablespoon chopped parsley

Beat the oil and lemon well together. Add the salt, pepper and parsley. Serve either in a side dish or pour directly over the fish.

Olive oil and vinegar dressing (*ladhóxidho*)

This dressing is used with lettuce, tomato and boiled courgette salads and with boiled wild greens (*hórta*).

1 tablespoon olive oil
1 tablespoon wine vinegar
salt and pepper

Mix well and pour over salad.

Tomato sauce I (*sáltsa domátas*)

An easily made sauce with many variations, it is used with pasta and rice, and sometimes meat-balls and omelettes.

1 kg (2 lb) ripe tomatoes (or 2 tablespoons tomato paste diluted in 3 cups of water)
1 onion, grated
2 tablespoons butter
½ teaspoon ground cinnamon
salt and pepper

Blanch and peel the tomatoes. Quarter them and put them through a coarse sieve. Melt the butter in a saucepan. Add the puréed tomatoes (or diluted tomato paste), grated onion, cinnamon, salt and pepper. Cover and simmer over low heat for about 30 minutes, until the sauce thickens and becomes creamy.

Tomato sauce II

1 kg (2lb) ripe tomatoes (or 2 tablespoons tomato paste)
1 onion, grated
2-3 cloves garlic finely sliced
3 sprigs parsley
3-4 sticks celery
3 tablespoons butter
1-2 cups chicken stock
salt and pepper

Blanch, peel, quarter and purée the tomatoes by passing them through a coarse sieve (as above). Alternatively, use tomato paste diluted in two cups of water. Melt the butter in a saucepan. Add the onion and garlic and sauté until just golden. Tie the celery and parsley together (Greek celery is very much finer than most) and add to the saucepan together with the tomatoes, salt and pepper. Cover and simmer gently for 15 minutes. Add the stock. Stir and cook for another 30 minutes. Remove the celery and parsley before serving.

In both varieties of the sauce, olive oil can be substituted for butter, with the advantage that the sauce can then be safely kept for up to a week in the fridge. Instead of the parsley and celery you could use a bay leaf and a sprig of basil, which should, however, be removed before serving. Another possibility is adding a grated carrot, which has the effect of thickening the sauce. Water and white wine could be used in place of the stock.

Tomato and minced meat sauce (*sáltsa domátas me kimá*)

½ cup olive oil or butter
1 onion, grated
2 cloves garlic finely chopped
½kg (1 lb) minced veal
1 large tin tomatoes
1 tablespoon sugar
1 tablespoon tomato paste diluted in 1 cup water
1 bay leaf
1 sprig basil (optional)
1 wineglass white wine (optional)
salt and pepper

Sauté the onion and garlic in oil or butter until golden brown. Add the minced meat and cook, stirring, for 10 minutes. Break up the tomatoes and add along with the rest of the ingredients. Cook over low heat for about one hour, stirring occasionally. Serve with pasta or rice.

White sauce (*sáltsa besamél*)

4 level tablespoons butter
6 level tablespoons flour
2 cups warm milk
salt and white pepper
pinch of nutmeg
1-2 egg yolks (optional)

Melt the butter in a small heavy-bottomed saucepan over a low heat. Be careful not to let it burn. Gradually add in the flour, stirring with a wooden spoon to keep the texture smooth. Add the milk – pre-warmed – a little at a time, stirring continuously to prevent the formation of lumps. Remove from the fire and fold in the egg yolks, lightly beaten (if used). Season to taste.

These quantities will give about two cups of white sauce of medium thickness. To make more, simply increase the quantities proportionately.

White sauce can be made thicker or thinner to suit different requirements by varying the quantity of flour used. This recipe will give the right consistency for use with *pastítsio* or *moussakás*, (see pages 115 and 120). For a thicker sauce for pies, use 8 tablespoons of flour instead of 6. For a thinner sauce for use with soups and mixed with other sauces, use 3 tablespoons of butter and 3-4 tablespoons of flour.

STARTERS AND SALADS

Starters or appetizers, in Greek, are called *mezédhes* (singular: *mezés*). As explained elsewhere (see page 86), the idea of courses, or at least one plate of everything per person, is alien to Greek eating habits. A selection of *mezédhes* is placed on the table and everyone shares them. And although each person normally receives an individual portion of the main course, the starters very often remain on the table to be picked at throughout the meal. The same applies to salads, especially when eating out.

Many of the starters described here are relatively straightforward. In summer, particularly, when the heat reduces your appetite anyway, a selection of them, perhaps accompanied by some fruit, makes a varied and satisfying meal without the need for a main course.

Aubergine or Eggplant dip (*melitzanosaláta*)

1 kg (2 lb) medium-size aubergines, preferably fláskes (*see page 21*).
juice of 1 lemon
1 tablespoon vinegar
1 cup olive oil
1 small onion, grated
1 clove garlic, crushed (optional)
a little pepper and salt

Wash the aubergines and put them under the grill for 15 minutes on each side. Alternatively, cook them in a moderate oven for about one hour. When cool, slice them in two and scoop out the flesh, discarding as many seeds as possible. Place the pieces in a colander, sprinkle with salt and allow to stand for half an hour. Press the flesh with a fork to remove some of the juice. Then place in a blender, or mash well with a fork, add the lemon juice and blend. Gradually add the oil, onion and garlic, blending until all the ingredients have been thoroughly absorbed. The dip should be thick and rather coarse in texture. Mix in the vinegar at the end.

Melitzanosaláta is served either chilled or at room temperature and can be garnished with parsley and black olives.

Aubergines or Eggplants, fried (*melitzánes tiganités*)

1 kg (2 lb) aubergines — either the long or round variety (see page 21)
2 tablespoons flour
1 egg, well beaten
1/8 teaspoon bicarbonate of soda
salt and white pepper
a little water
oil for frying

Cut the aubergines into thin slices and place them in a colander. Sprinkle with salt and allow to stand for at least half an hour to draw the bitterness from them. Press lightly with a fork to squeeze out some of the fluid and pat dry.

Prepare a thick batter by mixing the flour with a little water, bicarbonate of soda and the beaten egg. Season with salt and pepper. Dip each slice of aubergine into the batter and fry quickly in very hot oil until crisp and golden. Best eaten immediately. Serve with *skordhaliá*.

Beetroot salad (*padzária saláta*)

A winter salad, it is always served with an oil and vinegar dressing, and sometimes with *skordhaliá* as well.

1 bunch of whole, uncooked beetroots
oil and vinegar dressing
salt

Top and tail the beetroots, discarding the root ends. Separate the stalks and leaves. Wash the roots carefully and place in a saucepan with plenty of water. Bring slowly to the boil. In the meantime, wash the stalks and leaves and add them to the pot with the roots after they have been cooking for about half an hour. Cook for another 5 minutes, then drain in a colander. Peel and slice the roots, and cut the stalks and leaves into pieces about 4cm (1½in) long. Serve lukewarm or cold in a shallow dish, seasoned with the oil and vinegar dressing.

Black-eyed bean salad (*fasólia mavromátika*)

¼kg (½lb) black-eyed beans
1 small onion, finely chopped
4 tablespoons olive oil
juice of ½ lemon
salt
parsley

Place the beans in salted water and bring to the boil. Cook for approximately half an hour. Drain in a colander and place in a shallow salad bowl. Pour over the oil and lemon juice. Sprinkle with salt and finely chopped parsley. Serve at room temperature, as a salad or *mezés*.

Cabbage salad (*lahanosaláta*)

Cheap and plentiful in the winter months, cabbage makes the most popular winter salad.

6-8 tender cabbage leaves, finely shredded
1 large carrot, grated
a few capers
oil and lemon dressing (see page 99)

Combine the cabbage, carrot and capers in a salad bowl. Pour over the oil and lemon dressing. Toss, and serve.

Cauliflower salad (*kounoupídhi saláta*)

1 cauliflower head
salt
oil and lemon dressing (see page 99)

Discard the stem and outer leaves of the cauliflower and scrape off any blemishes. Boil the cauliflower, either whole or cut into four or five pieces, in salted water for 5-8 minutes. Do not allow it to become soft and mushy. Serve cold with the oil and lemon dressing.

If preferred, the cauliflower can be steamed.

Cheese, fried (*saganáki*)

Saganáki is often served as a *mezés* at the *ouzerí* or taverna. It is tasty and very easy to prepare. It makes a good quick snack or a light dinner, accompanied by salad and fruit.

¼kg (½lb) hard cheese: kefalotíri, graviéra *or* kaséri
2 tablespoons flour
3 tablespoons butter or olive oil
juice of ½ lemon

Cut the cheese into slices 1cm (½in) thick. Sprinkle the slices with water and dust with flour. Heat the butter or oil in a frying pan and fry the cheese for 1-2 minutes on each side. Serve immediately, sprinkled with lemon juice.

Saganáki can be served plain, with sausages, or with an egg. To serve with an egg: as soon as you have turned the slices of cheese over in the pan, break an egg over them, then cover and cook until the egg is done.

Courgettes or Zucchini, boiled (*kolokíthia vrastá*)

1kg (2lb) small, firm courgettes
salt
oil and lemon or oil and vinegar dressing (see page 99)

Wash the courgettes. Top and tail and scrape them lightly. Place them in plenty of unsalted boiling water and cook for about 15 minutes. The secret is not to overcook them; they should still be a little hard. Drain and salt to taste. Serve cold, in a shallow dish with the oil and lemon or oil and vinegar dressing.

Courgettes or Zucchini, fried (*kolokithákia tiganitá*)

A favourite *mezés*, *kolokithákia tiganitá* cooked properly are crisp and truly delicious. The secret is to slice the courgettes very thin and fry them in very hot oil — it should just be beginning to smoke. Otherwise, they don't cook properly or else become soggy and tasteless.

½kg (1lb) courgettes
2 tablespoons flour
1 egg, well beaten with a fork
salt and white pepper
⅛ teaspoon bicarbonate of soda
a little water
oil for frying

Top and tail and wash the courgettes. Cut into very thin slices. Make a batter with the egg, bicarbonate of soda, flour and water, and season with pepper and a pinch of salt. Dip the slices of courgette in the batter. Fry briefly in smoking hot oil until golden and crisp. Eat immediately, either as a *mezés* (with *tzatzíki* or *skordhaliá*) or as an accompaniment to meat or fish dishes.

Eggs, scrambled with tomatoes (*strapatsádha*)

A simple dish, but very good when made with nice ripe tomatoes. It can be served as a *mezés* or the main course of a light summer dinner.

2 ripe tomatoes
4 eggs, beaten lightly with a fork
3 tablespoons olive oil
salt and black pepper

Blanch, peel and slice the tomatoes. Place them in a non-stick frying pan with a little salt and cook them in their own juice over low heat for about 5 minutes. Add the oil and pepper and cook for a further 2 minutes. Pour in the beaten eggs and cook slowly, stirring with a wooden spoon, for 2-3 minutes until the eggs are cooked but still soft and creamy. The consistency should be that of scrambled eggs. Serve immediately.

Less common, but just as good, is *strapatsádha* with courgettes instead of tomatoes. To prepare: substitute two large courgettes for the tomatoes. Clean and cut them into thin round slices. Salt and fry in hot oil for 5 minutes, then add the pepper and eggs.

Fish roe dip (*taramosaláta*)

Taramosaláta was traditionally eaten during the Lenten fast when meat was off-limits for the true believer. It is now served by tavernas throughout the year. It makes an excellent *mezés* or dip to be served with drinks. The *taramás*, or smoked fish roe, can be bought at the grocer's where it is sold by the weight.

¼kg (½lb) stale bread
*3-4 rusks (*friganiés Elíte *serve the purpose well)*
*110g (¼lb) fish roe (*taramás*)*
1 small onion, grated
1 cup olive oil
juice of 1 large lemon
1 tablespoon vinegar (optional)
parsley and black olives

Rinse the roe under running water to remove some of the salt. Cut off the bread crusts and soak the bread in water for 5 minutes together with the rusks. Squeeze dry, and place the bread, rusks and roe in a blender. Beat together, adding the olive oil and lemon juice a little at a time. Beat until the paste is creamy and smooth and the texture light and fluffy. Add in the grated onion with two tablespoons of water and the vinegar (if used) and mix well. Serve on a flat dish, garnished with parsley and black olives.

Green bean salad (*fasolákia saláta*)

*½kg (1lb) French or bobby beans (*fasolákia*)*
oil and vinegar or oil and lemon dressing

Wash and trim the beans. Place in unsalted boiling water and cook for about half an hour. The beans should be tender, but still firm. Drain and cool. Toss with the dressing of your choice and serve cold either as a salad or as a starter.

Lettuce and tomato salad (*saláta maróuli ke domáta*)

1 Cos lettuce
2 tomatoes
oil and lemon or oil and vinegar dressing

Remove the outer leaves and shred the lettuce into very thin strips. Place in a colander and wash in plenty of water. Pat dry. Slice the tomatoes and mix with the lettuce in a salad bowl. Toss with dressing.

A green pepper, spring onions, dill or rocket make a good addition to this salad.

Mixed salad (*horiátiki*)

Horiátiki, or Greek or village salad as it is often called on taverna menus, is the summer salad par excellence. Eaten with fresh bread, it makes a meal in itself.

3 large firm tomatoes
½ large cucumber, peeled and sliced
1 onion, sliced
1 thick slice féta *cheese, crumbled*
½ green pepper, cut in thin strips
black olives
oregano
salt and pepper
olive oil

Remove the hard part of the core of the tomatoes and cut the tomatoes into wedges. Place in a salad bowl with the onion, cheese, olives, cucumber and green pepper. Season to taste with oregano, salt and pepper. Pour over the olive oil and toss.

Peppers, baked (*piperiés psités*)

Served as a *mezés* or salad, this is an interesting and simple dish to make.

6 large red or green peppers
1 cup olive oil
4 tablespoons vinegar or lemon juice
salt and pepper
1 clove of garlic, crushed (optional)

Bake the peppers in a hot oven until their skin turns black and they become quite soft. It normally takes about half an hour, but the time varies according to their size. Drop them in cold water. When they are cool enough to handle, remove the burnt skin and the stems. Slit the peppers along one side and open them out so as to remove the seeds. Slice them lengthwise and place in a shallow bowl. Pour over the oil and vinegar (or lemon) dressing together with the crushed garlic, if you are using it. Serve at room temperature.

It is a pity to omit the garlic, for it adds piquancy and bite to the recipe. Peppers prepared in this fashion will keep for several days in the fridge, and the longer they marinate the tastier they become.

Potato salad (*patatasaláta*)

4 medium-size potatoes
2 hard-boiled eggs, sliced
8-10 black olives
1 onion, chopped
parsley or oregano
capers
1 carrot, sliced (optional)
oil and vinegar dressing
salt and pepper

Wash the potatoes and cut them in half. Boil in plenty of salted water until tender. Drain and cool. Remove the skins and slice them or chop them into small cubes. Place in a salad bowl with the eggs, carrot, olives, capers and onion. Pour over the dressing and season to taste. Sprinkle with chopped parsley or oregano. Toss and serve cold.

Tomato salad (*domatosaláta*)

In summertime, when lettuce is not easily obtainable, tomato is the basic salad ingredient. Be sure to buy tomatoes that are properly ripe but still firm. The very red ones that have turned slightly soft are fine for cooking, but have a musty taste when eaten raw.

3 large ripe, firm tomatoes, cut into wedges
1 onion, sliced
salt and oregano
olive oil

Cut the tomatoes in half and cut out the hard part of the core before slicing them into wedges. Place the wedges in a salad bowl. Add the onion and season to taste with salt. Pour over a liberal amount of olive oil and sprinkle with a pinch of oregano.

Nothing could be easier … or tastier!

Tomato and cucumber salad (*angourodomáta saláta*)

3 large tomatoes, cut into wedges
½ cucumber, peeled and sliced
1 green pepper, cut into thin strips
salt
oil and vinegar dressing

Mix the ingredients together in a salad bowl and season with a little salt. Pour over the oil and vinegar dressing and toss.

Wild green salad (*hórta*)

1 kg (2lb) hórta *(alternatively,* vlíta *or* radhíkia*)*
oil and lemon or oil and vinegar dressing
salt

Wash and clean the *hórta*. Cook in unsalted boiling water for 20 minutes. Drain and add salt. Serve cold, with the oil and lemon or oil and vinegar dressing.

Yoghurt and garlic dip (*tzatzíki*)

The most popular and widely obtainable taverna *mezés*, and very simple to make.

¼kg (½lb) thick, strained yoghurt
2-3 cloves of garlic, crushed
½ small cucumber
1 tablespoon olive oil (optional)

Wash and grate the cucumber coarsely. Place the yoghurt in a bowl. Stir in the garlic, cucumber and oil and serve.

SOUPS AND PULSES

Pulses, or *óspria* as they are called in Greek, have been an important part of the Greeks' diet since ancient times. The main reason obviously is that they are very cheap and easy to produce on Greece's infertile soil. But they can also be extremely tasty and nourishing. There is nothing like a good *fasoládha* – bean soup – for keeping out the cold on a winter's day. And in fact the eating of *óspria* is particularly associated with winter and the fasting in Lent.

For all their cheapness, *fasoládha* and lentil soup in particular remain great favourites in all classes of society – though there is a foolish tendency among the newly rich to disdain all *óspria* as the food of the poor. It is a standing joke that the army is fed exclusively on a diet of beans, with the expected consequences!

Chick pea soup (*revíthia sóupa*)

½kg (1lb) chick peas
2 level tablespoons bicarbonate of soda
3 small onions, finely chopped
½ cup olive oil
1 lemon
salt

Wash the chick peas and leave to soak in cold water overnight. Drain and sprinkle with the bicarbonate of soda. Mix and leave to stand for approximately an hour. Then rinse well in plenty of hot water. Try to get rid of as much of the pea skins as possible. Rinse a second time in lots of cold water.

Place the chick peas in a saucepan, cover with water and bring to the boil. Add the onions and cook until soft. Reduce the heat. Pour in the oil, season with salt and simmer until very soft. Serve hot with lemon.

Egg and lemon soup with chicken (*sóupa avgolémono me kotópoulo*)

1 medium-size chicken
3-4 sticks celery
3-4 carrots
1-2 green peppers
2 onions, whole
1 cup rice
2 eggs
juice of 2 lemons
pepper and salt

Wash and clean the chicken and place in a large saucepan together with all the vegetables. Cover with water, bring to the boil and cook for 1-1½ hours, depending on the size of the chicken. It is ready when the leg can be easily separated from the body. During the cooking, skim the broth.

Remove the chicken and vegetables from the saucepan, drain and put in a serving dish. Strain the broth and return it to the pan with the addition of just enough water to make four cups of liquid. Pour in one cup of rice and cook for 20 minutes, then remove from the heat. Beat the eggs well with the lemon juice. Put one tablespoon of lukewarm broth in the mixture and stir. Add two further tablespoons of broth and mix well. Pour the egg mixture into the broth very slowly, stirring continuously. It is important that the eggs should not cook and separate, so you have to be careful to maintain the right temperature all the time. Return to low heat for 1-2 minutes before serving.

This is a very light soup, often served to those recovering from illness. You can either keep the chicken and vegetables separate and have them as a main course, or bone the bird and add the meat and vegetables to the soup.

Giant or butter beans in tomato sauce (*fasólia yígandes plakí*)

½kg (1lb) butter beans (yígandes)
2 small onions, sliced
2-3 cloves of garlic, chopped

1 cup olive oil
parsley
salt and pepper
3-4 medium-size tomatoes, blanched, peeled and cut into small cubes

Leave the beans to soak in cold water overnight. Rinse, cover with cold water and boil for 45 minutes. Rinse again and set aside.

Sauté the onions and garlic in the olive oil until golden brown. Add the tomatoes and parsley, two teaspoonfuls of salt and a little pepper. Cook for about 30 minutes, stirring until all the ingredients are well blended.

Put the beans in an oven-proof dish, pour over the sauce and cook in a pre-heated moderate oven for 40 minutes.

Giant or butter beans and tomato stew (*fasólia yígandes yiahní*)

½kg (1lb) butter beans (yígandes)
1 cup olive oil
3 tablespoons finely chopped parsley
2-3 onions, sliced
½ tablespoon tomato paste diluted with 1 cup water
salt and pepper

Wash the beans and leave to soak overnight in fresh water. Rinse, return to saucepan, cover with cold water and bring to the boil. Drain off the water and add the oil, parsley, onions, and a little salt and pepper to the beans. Cook until the onion is soft and golden, stirring occasionally with a wooden spoon. Add two cups of warm water. Cover and simmer gently for about one hour, before adding the diluted tomato paste. Continue cooking, stirring occasionally, until the beans are tender and the water has evaporated.

Haricot bean soup (*fasoládha*)

½kg (1lb) haricot beans
2 medium-size onions
1 cup tomato juice
3-4 sticks celery, chopped
6 carrots, scraped and finely chopped
½ cup of olive oil
1 tablespoon salt
1 teaspoon sugar
6 peppercorns

Cover the beans with water and bring to the boil. Cook for two minutes, then leave to stand for one hour. Drain and discard the water. Place the beans, vegetables, tomato juice, sugar and peppercorns in a large saucepan and add ten cups of water. Cook for about 1½ hours, adding more water if necessary (some beans will absorb a lot of liquid). 10 minutes before the cooking is over, add the oil and salt to the soup. Mix well and serve hot.

Lentil soup (*fakés*)

Like *fasoládha*, *fakés* is a favourite winter dish in Greece. It is usually served with plenty of fresh bread, black olives and tinned sardines.

½kg (1 lb) lentils
1 onion
½ cup olive oil
2 teaspoons salt
1 bay leaf
3 tablespoons vinegar
1 tablespoon tomato paste (optional)

Boil the lentils in plenty of water for one minute. Take them off the heat, and discard the water. Rinse the lentils and replace in a saucepan with the onion – whole – a bay leaf and seven cups of water. Allow to boil ½-1 hour, adding more water if necessary. (Some lentils cook much more rapidly than others.) Add the tomato paste, oil and salt and allow to boil for a further 10 minutes. Remove from the heat, add the vinegar and stir. The *fakés* is ready to serve.

Lentils, yellow (*fáva*)

½kg (1 lb) yellow lentils
2 small onions
½ cup olive oil
juice of 1 lemon
parsley
2 teaspoons salt
pepper

Wash the lentils. Place in a saucepan and cover with water. As the water begins to boil, remove the froth and add one onion cut into four pieces. Allow to boil on low heat for about one hour. Pass the lentils through a sieve and return them to the saucepan with half the oil, salt and pepper. Boil for a further 5 minutes stirring continuously. Serve cold in a shallow dish with the remainder of the onion, finely sliced, the parsley, lemon juice and oil.

Vegetable soup (*hortósoupa*)

2 medium-size potatoes
2-3 onions
4-5 carrots
1 stick celery
2-3 ripe tomatoes, peeled
4 tablespoons oil or butter

parsley	*1 tablespoon salt*
1 teaspoon sugar	*pepper*

Wash and clean all the vegetables and chop them finely. Sauté the onions in hot oil or butter until they soften. Add the potatoes and carrots, and cook – stirring – until they begin to soften. Add the rest of the vegetables, seasoning, and sugar. Cover with water and simmer gently for about 1½ hours. Either pass the vegetables through a coarse sieve and warm again before serving, or serve the soup as it is.

SAVOURY PIES, PASTA AND RICE DISHES

The savoury pies described here are among the more interesting recipes in the Greek repertoire. All are made with the very thin leaf-like *fílo* pastry, which can be bought ready-made at the grocer's or supermarket.

Cheese pie (*tirópita*)

½kg (1 lb) féta	*½kg (1 lb)* fílo *pastry*
½kg (1 lb) graviéra, *grated*	*pepper*
6 eggs, beaten	*nutmeg or mint*
1 l (1¾pt) thick white sauce (see page 101)	*butter*

Mash the *féta* and the grated *graviéra* together in a bowl with a fork. Pour over the white sauce and mix well. Add the eggs, nutmeg or mint and work well together with a wooden spoon.

Spread half the *fílo* pastry sheets in a buttered baking dish, brushing the top one with butter. Pour in the filling and cover with the remaining pastry sheets. Score the surface of the *fílo* lightly in one direction – three lines is enough. Brush with butter, sprinkle with a little water and cook in a pre-heated moderate oven for about three quarters of an hour.

Before serving, cut the *tirópita* into squares.

Chicken pie (*kotópita*)

A delicious dish and a good way to dispose of any chicken leftovers which have turned dry and unappetising. If you don't have enough chicken you can add some cooked macaroni to make the pie-filling go further.

1 medium-size chicken, cooked
4 cups thick white sauce (see page 101)
6 eggs
½kg (1 lb) fílo *pastry sheets*
pinch of nutmeg
butter
pepper

Remove the skin from the cooked chicken and cut the meat into small pieces. Prepare a white sauce and allow to cool. Beat the eggs lightly with a fork and fold into the white sauce when cool. Mix the sauce and chicken pieces.

Spread half the pastry sheets in a buttered baking dish, one on top of the other. Brush the top sheet with a little melted butter and spread the chicken mixture over it, smoothing it out with a fork. Layer the remaining pastry sheets on the top. Brush the surface with a little more butter. Score lightly and cook in a pre-heated moderate oven for about half an hour, until golden brown and crisp.

Courgette or Zucchini pie (*kolokithópita*)

1½kg (3 lb) courgettes
½kg (1 lb) fílo *pastry*
½kg (1 lb) féta *and* graviéra, *grated and mixed*
1 onion, sliced
6 eggs, beaten
1 cup olive oil or butter
*2 tablespoons semolina (*simigdáli*)*
pinch of mint
salt and pepper

Brown the onion in olive oil or butter. Add the courgettes, grated or cut into small pieces, and cook for 3-4 minutes, turning on each side. Add the semolina and seasoning and cook for a further 5 minutes, stirring meanwhile. Remove from the heat. Add the cheese and eggs and mix well. Spread half of the *fílo* pastry sheets in a buttered baking dish and brush the top sheet with a little butter. Spread the courgette mixture evenly over the pastry. Cover with the remaining *fílo* sheets, brush with butter and score the surface lightly in one direction. Cook in a preheated moderate oven for about half an hour, until crisp.

Leeks with rice (*prasórizo*)

6-8 leeks
1 cup rice
1 cup olive oil
½ teaspoon tomato paste
1 teaspoon sugar
1 tablespoon chopped dill
2 tablespoons currants
2 tablespoons pine-nuts
pinch of cinnamon
salt and pepper

Remove and discard the coarse outer skin and leaves of the leeks. Wash the remainder, drain and cut into pieces about 5cm (2in) long. Place in a saucepan without any water and cook over low heat for 10 minutes. Stir in all the other ingredients except for the rice and add two cups of water. Cook over a moderate heat until the leeks are just tender. Bring the water to the boil, and shower in the rice. Stir once and cook covered for 10 minutes until most of the water has been absorbed by the rice. Remove from the fire. Place a clean cloth over the saucepan, cover with the lid and leave to stand until all the water has been absorbed.

Macaroni, baked with minced meat (*pastítsio*)

½kg (1 lb) macaroni
*½kg (1 lb) minced beef (*kimá*)*
¼kg (½lb) grated cheese (you can use kefalotíri, kefalograviéra *or a mixture of cheeses)*
1 onion, finely chopped
1 small glass white wine
1 cup olive oil
3 tablespoons butter
1 small tin tomatoes
½l (1 pt) white sauce (see page 101)
4 eggs
1 teaspoon sugar
2 cloves
pinch of nutmeg

Sauté the onion in hot oil until soft. Add the tin of tomatoes and cook together for 5 minutes, then add the minced meat, salt, pepper, cloves and sugar. Leave to cook on medium heat for half an hour.

Cook the macaroni in a large saucepan of boiling water for 12 minutes, then drain and rinse in cold water. Butter a large baking dish. Add the macaroni and mix with half the grated cheese.

Prepare a white sauce as directed. When it has cooled, fold in four beaten eggs and a pinch of nutmeg, and mix well.

Add three tablespoons of the white sauce to the macaroni and cheese. Mix in well, then spread the mixture evenly over the baking dish. Pour in the minced meat sauce and cover with the remaining white sauce. Sprinkle over with the remaining cheese, and place a few squares of butter on top. Cook in a moderately hot oven until brown and crusty; it should take about 30 minutes.

Pastítsio can be served hot or tepid.

Pilaf in the Milanese style (*piláfi milanéza*)

2 cups rice
4½ cups beef or chicken stock
½ cup white wine
1 onion, thinly sliced
4 tablespoons butter
½ cup Parmesan cheese, grated
salt

Heat the butter in a frying pan and sauté the onion until soft and golden. Pour in the rice and cook together, stirring, for 2 minutes, then add the wine. When the steam subsides, turn off the heat.

In another pan, bring the stock to the boil. Add the rice, cover and cook until all the water is absorbed. Serve topped with a little butter and the Parmesan cheese.

Pilaf with tomato sauce (*piláfi me saltsa domátas*)

2 cups rice
2 tablespoons butter
tomato sauce (see page 99)
salt

Cook the rice in five cups of boiling salted water. Drain and return to the pan. Pour over the melted butter and cook for 1-2 minutes, stirring. Served topped with tomato sauce.

Spaghetti with minced meat sauce (*makarónia me kimá*)

1 kg (2 lb) spaghetti
1 cup grated cheese
½ cup butter
tomato and minced meat sauce (see page 100)

Cook the spaghetti for 10-12 minutes in plenty of boiling salted water. Drain and return to the pan. Pour over the melted butter and toss. Put the spaghetti on a platter, sprinkle with cheese and pour the sauce over. Sprinkle some more cheese on top and serve.

Spaghetti with tomato sauce (*makarónia me sáltsa domátas*)

1 kg (2 lb) spaghetti
*1 cup grated cheese (*kefalotíri *or* kefalograviéra*)*
½ cup butter
tomato sauce (see page 99)

Cook the spaghetti for 10-12 minutes in plenty of boiling salted water. Drain and return to the pan. Pour over the melted butter and toss. Sprinkle with cheese and serve on a platter with a bowl of cheese and the tomato sauce.

Spinach pie (*spanakópita*)

1½kg (3lb) spinach (if fresh is not available, frozen may be used)
½kg (1lb) fílo pastry sheets
¼kg (½lb) feta cheese
6 eggs, beaten
salt and pepper
1 cup olive oil
1 onion, grated or finely chopped
3-4 sprigs dill

Clean and wash the spinach. Discard the stalks and cut the leaves into three. Place in a bowl with the onion, salt and dill. Allow to stand for 10-15 minutes. Put in a colander and press to get rid of the excess juice. Then mix the spinach in a bowl with the grated cheese, eggs, pepper and a quarter of the oil.

Oil a baking dish and spread half the pastry sheets on the bottom. Brush the top sheet with oil, and spread the spinach mixture over evenly. Cover with the remaining pastry sheets and lightly brush the uppermost one with oil. Lightly score the surface in one direction only and bake in a preheated moderate oven for about three quarters of an hour, until golden and crisp.

Cut into squares before serving.

Spanakópita may be eaten hot or cold, and keeps well in the fridge.

Spinach with rice (*spanakórizo*)

1½kg (3lb) spinach
1 cup rice
1 tablespoon tomato paste diluted in 1 cup water
1 cup olive oil
1 onion, sliced
salt and pepper

Wash the spinach in plenty of clean water and remove any tough stalks or yellow leaves. Cut the remainder in two. Heat the oil in a saucepan and sauté the onion until just soft, but still transparent. Add in the spinach and cook together for 5 minutes, stirring. Add the diluted tomato paste, plus a further 1½ cups of water and seasoning. Cover and simmer gently for 10 minutes. Bring to the boil and add the rice. Stir well with a wooden spoon, then cover and cook until the rice swells. When most of the water has been absorbed, remove from the fire, place a clean cloth over the pan, replace the lid and leave to stand for 10 minutes. Stir and serve.

VEGETABLE DISHES

Aubergines or Eggplants baked with tomatoes (*melitzánes imám bayaldí*)

1 kg (2 lb) aubergines – fláskes variety (see page 21)
1 cup olive oil
3 large tomatoes, sliced
1 teaspoon sugar
½ cup tomato juice
salt

Wash the aubergines. Cut off and discard the stems. Cut the aubergines into slices 2 cm (1 in) thick, sprinkle liberally with salt and allow to stand for about half an hour. The salt draws their natural bitterness and prevents blackening.

Squeeze the slices with your hands to extract some of the juice, then sauté lightly in hot oil until golden in colour. Place them side by side in a large baking dish and arrange slices of tomato on top of each piece. Season with salt, pepper and sugar. Pour over the tomato juice, the remaining oil and half a cup of water. Bake in a pre-heated moderate oven for about 45 minutes. Serve cold, as a starter or main course.

Beans with tomato and olive oil (*fasolákia ladherá*)

*1 kg (2 lb) fresh or frozen French or bobby beans (*fasolákia*)*
2 small onions, sliced
1 cup olive oil
4 tomatoes, peeled and chopped
parsley
2 teaspoons salt
pepper

Wash and string the beans, and cut them in two. Heat the oil in a saucepan and gently sauté the onions. Add the tomatoes, beans, parsley, a little pepper and two cups of water. Leave to cook over low heat for about an hour. Add salt 10 minutes before turning off the heat.

Like other *ladherá* dishes, this one can be eaten at room temperature or quite cold. Greeks usually prefer their *ladherá* to be cold.

Courgettes or Zucchini, stuffed (*kolokithákia yemistá*)

$1\frac{1}{2}$kg (3lb) medium-size courgettes
$\frac{1}{4}$kg ($\frac{1}{2}$lb) minced meat
2 tablespoons rice
2 small onions, grated or finely chopped
2 tomatoes, peeled, halved and sliced
1 cup olive oil
$\frac{1}{2}$ cup tomato juice
$\frac{1}{4}$ cup non-resinated white wine
1 teaspoon dried mint
salt and pepper

Wash, top and tail the courgettes, and place them in boiling water to cook for 3-4 minutes. Strain, and when cool enough to handle, split lengthwise and remove the pulp of each with a small spoon. Put half the pulp aside and discard the rest. Place the courgettes side by side in a well-greased baking dish..

Grate the courgette pulp and put it in a mixing bowl with the minced meat, rice, onion, mint, seasoning and a quarter of the olive oil. Mix well with a wooden spoon. Using a teaspoon, fill the hollowed out parts of the courgettes with the mixture. Cover with slices of tomato. Pour over the tomato juice, one cup of water, the wine and remaining oil. Sprinkle with salt and pepper. Cover with aluminium foil and bake in a preheated moderate oven for about one hour.

The recipe can also be made with a thick white sauce. If you wish to try, simply cover the stuffed courgettes with sauce instead of tomato slices, and cook.

Mixed vegetables in the oven (*briámi, tourlóu*)

$\frac{1}{2}$kg (1 lb) aubergines
1 kg (2lb) courgettes
2 green peppers
2 medium-size onions
4 medium-size tomatoes, peeled
2-3 sticks celery (optional)
2 cloves garlic
1 cup olive oil
parsley
salt and pepper

Wash, clean and cut all the vegetables into small, thick pieces. Mix together with the garlic, oil, seasoning and parsley. Spread in a baking dish and cook in a pre-heated moderate oven for about one hour. Alternatively, cook in a casserole for about half an hour, stirring occasionally.

Briámi may be eaten warm or cold and keeps well in the fridge. You can vary the vegetable ingredients according to season and taste. Potatoes, carrots, French beans – all go well, but it is better not to mix too many different vegetables in the same version of the recipe.

Moussakás

1 kg (2 lb) aubergines
½ kg (1 lb) potatoes
½ kg (1 lb) minced meat
2-3 tomatoes, peeled and chopped
1 onion, sliced
1 cup olive oil
½ glass tomato juice
¼ cup non-resinated white wine
½ cup grated cheese
8 cups white sauce (see page 101)
salt and pepper

Wash and peel the potatoes and cut into thin slices. Wash the aubergines and cut into thin round slices, discarding the stems. Sprinkle with salt and allow to stand for 30 minutes. Using half the olive oil, sauté the potatoes until they turn golden, then leave to drain in a colander. Squeeze the aubergines to extract some of the juice, rinse under running water and pat dry. Sauté lightly in hot oil. Strain and pat dry again. Arrange the potatoes and aubergines in alternate layers in a large buttered baking dish.

Heat the rest of the oil in another saucepan. Throw in the onion, tomatoes and minced meat and sauté for 5 minutes. Add the tomato juice, wine, seasoning and, if necessary, a little water and cook over low heat for about half an hour.

Spread the meat sauce on top of the layers of aubergine and potato. Top with white sauce mixed with grated cheese. Cook in a pre-heated moderate oven for about 45 minutes, until the top becomes golden brown.

Serve hot or at room temperature.

Okra, casseroled in oil (*bámies ladherés*)

1 kg (2 lb) fresh or frozen okra
1 tomato, peeled and sliced
2 onions, sliced
1 cup tomato juice
1 cup olive oil
vinegar
1 teaspoon sugar
salt and pepper

Wash the okra, trim the tops, and spread on a large dish. Sprinkle with vinegar and salt and allow to stand for an hour to let the slime draw off. Rinse well and strain.

Heat the oil in a large saucepan. Add the okra and onions and sauté until the okra begin to turn yellow. Add the tomato and tomato juice, a little water, seasoning and sugar and cook gently for about 45 minutes without stirring.

Bámies are eaten cold or at room temperature. Like other *ladherá* dishes, their taste is enhanced when they are left to marinate for a day or two in their sauce.

Peas in oil (*arakás ladherós*)

1 kg (2 lb) fresh or frozen peas
¼ kg (½ lb) fresh tomatoes or 1 tablespoon tomato paste diluted in 2 cups warm water
1 bunch spring onions, chopped
1 cup olive oil
3 tablespoons chopped dill
salt and pepper

If using fresh peas, shell, wash and strain them. Peel and slice the tomatoes finely. Sauté the onions in hot oil until soft. Add the peas and cook for 2-3 minutes, stirring. Add the tomatoes and seasoning. Cover and cook slowly until the peas are tender; (you can add a little water to the sauce if necessary). Cooking time is about 40 minutes.

Potato casserole with tomatoes and carrots (*patátes yiahní*)

1 kg (2 lb) potatoes
½ kg (1 lb) tomatoes, peeled and sliced, or 1 tablespoon tomato paste diluted in 1 cup water
2 cloves garlic, chopped
2 sticks celery, chopped
2 carrots, finely chopped
2-3 onions finely sliced
¾ cup olive oil
salt and pepper
oregano

Wash and peel the potatoes and cut into chunks. Leave in water. Heat the oil in a large saucepan, and sauté the onion until it turns soft and golden. Add the tomatoes or diluted paste, carrots, garlic, celery and seasoning. Cook together for 5 minutes, then add the potatoes and a little water, if necessary. Cover and cook on moderate heat for about 40 minutes.

Potatoes, roasted, with oregano (*patátes sto fóurno riganátes*)

1 kg (2 lb) potatoes
¾ cup olive oil
juice of 1 lemon
pinch of oregano
salt and pepper

Wash and peel the potatoes. Parboil in salted water for 10 minutes. Strain and cut into chunks – *kidhonátes*: like a half-moon. Season with salt and pepper and place in a baking dish. Pour over the oil and lemon juice. Sprinkle a pinch of oregano (not too much, for it will give the potatoes a bitter taste) and cook in a pre-heated moderate oven for 45 minutes to one hour.

Tomatoes and green peppers, stuffed (*domátes yemistés/piperiés yemistés*)

1 kg (2 lb) large tomatoes
½ kg (1 lb) green peppers
2 large onions, grated or finely chopped
1 cup rice
3 tablespoons pine-nuts
3 tablespoons sultanas
1 cup olive oil
½ cup tomato juice
a little parsley and mint
2 teaspoons sugar
salt and pepper

Wash the tomatoes, turn them upside down and cut off the bottoms for use as caps. Scoop out the pulp and seeds, leaving only the outer layer of the vegetable intact. Discard the seeds and set the pulp on one side. Cut the tops off the peppers, scoop out and discard the pith and seeds.

Place tomatoes and peppers side by side in a baking dish. Sprinkle the inside of each with a little salt and half the sugar and cover them with their caps.

Heat half the oil in a saucepan, and sauté the onion, chopped tomato pulp, parsley, mint and pine-nuts. Cook for 20 minutes, stirring occasionally, then add the rice, sultanas and seasoning. Cook together for another 5 minutes.

Fill the tomatoes and peppers with the rice mixture to about 1 cm (½in) below the top. Put their caps back on and pour over the tomato juice, the remaining oil, salt and sugar. Bake in a moderate oven for about an hour.

Yemistá, as stuffed tomatoes and peppers are called for short, definitely improve in taste when left to marinate for a day or two. They will keep for several days in the fridge, and can be eaten either cold or at room temperature.

FISH AND SEAFOOD

Baked fish (*psári psitó*)

The following fish are good for baking: gilthead bream, pandora, sea bream and the larger red mullet (see pages 38, 39, 40 and 41)

1 large fish
3 medium-size tomatoes, peeled and chopped, or 1 small tin of ready-peeled tomatoes
1 onion, sliced
juice of 1 lemon
1 cup olive oil
3 sprigs parsley
salt and pepper

Wash and clean the fish. Season with salt and pepper and place in an oiled baking dish with the tomatoes, onion and parsley. Baste well with oil and lemon juice. Bake in a moderate oven, about 20 minutes each side, basting frequently.

Boiled fish (*psári vrastó*)

Cod, dentex, sea-bass and sea bream are suitable fish for boiling (see pages 37, 38 and 41)

1 kg (2 lb) fish
3-4 medium-size potatoes
2 onions
3-4 carrots
3-4 sticks of celery
1 cup olive oil
juice of 1-2 lemons
salt and pepper

Wash and clean the fish, season with salt and pepper and leave to stand for half an hour.

Wash and clean all the vegetables. Cut the potatoes in half, unless they are very small. Chop the carrots, celery and onions. Place all the vegetables together in a large saucepan with the oil, seasoning and a cup of water. Cook over moderate heat for about 20 minutes. Place the fish on top of the vegetables. Pour over the lemon juice. Add 3-4 cups of water and cook for another 15-20 minutes. Serve.

Cod: fried salt cod with garlic sauce (*bakaliáros tiganitós me skordhaliá*)

1 kg (2 lb) dried salt cod
1 cup flour
1 egg
½ teaspoon bicarbonate of soda
1-2 cloves garlic
2 cups olive oil
skordhaliá sauce (see page 98)

Remove the skin from the cod and cut the flesh into pieces about 5 cm (2 in) square. Leave to soak in water for at least 12 hours, changing the water two or three times. Bone, drain and dry the fish.

Prepare a batter by mixing the flour with a little water, the bicarbonate of soda and the egg, beaten. Heat the oil in a deep pan and sauté the garlic until it turns golden, then remove from the pan. Dip each piece of cod in the batter and fry in the oil until crisp and golden. Serve hot or cold with *skordhaliá* and a salad.

Fried fish (*psári tiganitó*)

1 kg (2 lb) picarel, anchovies or sardines
flour
olive oil
juice of 1 or 2 lemons
salt and pepper

Wash the fish and dip in flour seasoned with salt and pepper. Fry in plenty of smoking hot oil until very crisp. Serve either hot or cold, with lemon wedges.

Grilled fish (*psári sti skára*)

Suitable fish for grilling are gilt-head bream, dentex, pandora and the larger red mullet.

4 medium-size fish, fresh or frozen
few sprigs of fresh fennel or 1 tablespoon dried fennel
½ cup olive oil
juice of 1 lemon
salt and pepper

Wash and clean the fish. Season with salt and pepper and leave to drain. Put some salt, pepper and fennel in their bellies and baste with a mixture of olive oil and lemon juice. Grill in the oven or on a barbecue over charcoal, basting frequently. If using a barbecue, be very careful when you turn the fish over, so they do not stick to the bars of the grill and disintegrate. It is best to oil the bars first. Serve immediately.

Mussels with pilaf (*mídhia me piláfi*)

1 kg (2 lb) mussels
1 onion, sliced
½ cup white wine
1 cup olive oil
2 cups rice
1 tablespoon tomato paste diluted in 1 cup of water
2 tablespoons finely chopped parsley
salt and pepper

Wash the mussels in several changes of water, scrubbing each shell carefully to remove the grit and sand. Place in a saucepan with a little water and cook for a few minutes until the shells open. Remove the mussels from the pan and shell them. Discard any mussels that have not opened. Strain the broth, preferably through a fine muslin cloth, and set aside.

Heat the oil in a saucepan and sauté the onion until golden. Add the mussels and sauté for a couple of minutes, before pouring in the wine. When the steam subsides, add the tomato paste and seasoning and cook, stirring with a wooden spoon for 3-4 minutes, until the sauce thickens. Add the mussel broth and four cups of water. Stir and bring to the boil, then add the rice. Cover and simmer gently until the rice is cooked and the liquid has been absorbed.

Serve hot, garnished with parsley.

Octopus in wine (*ohtapódhi krasáto*)

1½kg (3lb) fresh or frozen octopus
2-3 onions, thinly sliced
4 medium-size tomatoes, peeled and sliced
1-2 cloves garlic
parsley, chopped
3 tablespoons currants
3 tablespoons pine-nuts
1 cup olive oil
½ cup red or white wine
black pepper

Wash and clean the octopus. Simmer gently in a covered saucepan for 15 minutes without any water; their own juice is sufficient. The flesh will turn a rosy pink. Strain, and slice the tentacles into small pieces. Throw away the head and beak.

Heat the oil in a saucepan and sauté the onions for 3-4 minutes, then add the octopus and garlic and cook together for a few minutes. Pour in the wine, cover and simmer gently until the wine has evaporated. Add the tomatoes, stir, and continue to cook on low heat until the sauce thickens and the octopus is tender – about 40 minutes, for a small to medium-size octopus. Add the currants, parsley, pine-nuts and pepper 5 minutes before the end of cooking.

Serve hot or at room temperature with rice or pasta.

This is another dish that improves if you leave it to marinate for a few hours.

Prawns, boiled (*garídhes vrastés*)

¼kg (½lb) prawns
1 tablespoon vinegar
coarse salt

Wash the prawns in plenty of water and place in a small saucepan with the vinegar, salt and half a cup of water. Cover and simmer gently over low heat, shaking the pan occasionally to ensure even cooking. Cooking time is about 10 minutes. When the prawns have cooled, shell them and serve with *ladholémono* sauce (see page 99) or mayonnaise, as a starter.

Sardines, baked (*sardhéles sto fóurno*)

1kg (2lb) sardines
2 medium-size onions, sliced
2 green peppers, cut lengthwise
3 tomatoes, peeled and sliced
black olives, pitted
1 cup olive oil
½ cup white wine
salt and pepper

Wash and clean the sardines. Cut off the heads and throw out. Leave to drain well.

Heat the oil in a frying pan and sauté the onions and peppers until soft. Add the tomatoes and seasoning and cook over high heat for 5 minutes, stirring frequently. Pour in the wine and stir. When the steam subsides, remove from the fire and pour the sauce into a baking dish. Place the sardines and olives in the dish and cook in a moderate pre-heated oven for half an hour. Serve hot or cold, with a tomato salad.

Squid, fried (*kalamarákia tiganitá*)

1kg (2lb) baby squid, fresh or frozen
lemon wedges
flour
salt and pepper
olive oil

When they are no more than 4cm (1½in) long, the very small squid can be fried whole. Anything bigger – and this is what you are most likely to get – will need cleaning and cutting into smaller pieces.

Clean by pulling the tentacles away from the body or sac. Cut the tentacles just above the eyes and throw away the rest of the head. Squeeze out the small hard beak. Remove the transparent backbone from the sac and clean out the inside of the sac thoroughly. Peel off the outer, often brownish, skin. Rinse sac and tentacles in several changes of water.

If the heads are small, leave them intact. Otherwise, cut in two. Cut the sacs into narrow rings. Dip rings and tentacles in flour seasoned with salt and pepper. Put about 2½cm (1in) of oil in the bottom of a saucepan and heat until it begins to smoke. Put the pieces of squid carefully into the pan so as not to splash scalding oil, and fry until crisp and golden. Don't put too many pieces in at once. Drain on kitchen paper and serve hot with lemon wedges.

Squid in wine sauce (*kalamária krasáta*)

1kg (2lb) squid
3 small onions
½ cup olive oil
1 cup white wine
1 small tin peeled tomatoes
1 clove garlic (optional)
parsley, chopped
salt and pepper

Clean and wash the squid thoroughly as for the previous recipe. Drain well. Heat the oil in a large saucepan and sauté the onions and squid together, whole, for a few minutes. Add the wine. When it has evaporated, add the tomatoes, seasoning, parsley and garlic. Cook until tender. Serve cold, with rice.

MEAT AND POULTRY

Chicken casserole with okra (*kotópoulo me bámies*)

1 chicken
½kg (1lb) fresh or frozen okra
2 medium-size onions, sliced
2 cloves garlic
2 cups tomato juice
1 cup olive oil or butter
1 teaspoon sugar
vinegar
salt and pepper

Wash the okra and trim off the tops. Spread on a large plate and rinse with vinegar. Allow to stand for one hour.

Cut the chicken into pieces and season with salt and pepper. Heat half the oil or butter in a large saucepan and sauté the garlic and onions until soft. Add the chicken pieces and cook together for a few minutes, turning the chicken pieces over once or twice. Pour in the tomato juice and sugar and leave to simmer on low heat for one hour.

Rinse the okra thoroughly in fresh water and drain. Heat the remainder of the oil or butter and sauté the okra. Add some broth from the chicken and simmer over low heat without stirring until quite tender – about 30-40 minutes.

Serve the chicken on a serving dish garnished with the okra, either hot or at room temperature.

Chicken casserole with tomato sauce (*kotópoulo kokinistó*)

1 large chicken
½kg (1lb) ripe tomatoes, peeled and finely sliced or 1 tablespoon tomato paste diluted in 1 cup of water
¼ cup red or white wine
½ cup butter
1 stick cinnamon
2 cloves
salt and pepper

Wash, clean and dry the chicken. Season inside and out with salt and pepper. Heat the butter in a large saucepan. Put in the chicken and sauté well, turning it on all sides until the skin is golden all over. Then pour in the wine and when the steam has subsided, add the tomatoes or paste, cinnamon and cloves. Cover and cook slowly, adding a little water from time to time. Cooking time varies from 1½ to 2 hours, depending on the size of the bird (it is ready when the leg separates easily from the body). There should be just a little thick sauce left at the end of cooking.

Serve with French fries, potato purée or pilaf.

Chicken, roast, with potatoes (*kotópoulo sto fóurno me patátes*)

1 chicken
1kg (2lb) medium-size potatoes
juice of 1 lemon
½ cup olive oil
1 teaspoon oregano
salt and pepper

Wash, clean and dry the chicken. Season inside and out with salt and pepper. Truss the wings and legs, and place in a roasting pan. Brush with lemon juice.

Wash the potatoes and parboil for 10 minutes, then peel and quarter them. Arrange in the roasting pan around the chicken and season with salt and pepper. Sprinkle both chicken and potatoes with oregano and pour the oil over them. Cook in a pre-heated moderate oven for about 1½ hours, until the chicken is crisp and golden brown. Baste regularly during cooking.

Lamb casserole, with fresh peas (*arní me araká*)

1 kg (2 lb) shoulder or leg of lamb
1½ kg (3 lb) fresh young peas
½ kg (1 lb) ripe tomatoes. peeled and sliced
1 tablespoon finely chopped dill
½ cup butter
salt and pepper

Pass the tomatoes through a coarse sieve to make a pulp. Wash and dry the lamb and season with salt and pepper. Place in a casserole with the butter and a third of the tomato pulp. Put in a pre-heated moderate oven.

Shell, wash and strain the peas. Add the remaining tomato pulp and 1½ cups of water to the lamb. As the juice starts to boil, add the peas and dill and some salt and pepper. Cook slowly for about one hour.

Lamb cutlets, grilled or barbecued (*païdhákia*)

1 kg (2 lb) lamb cutlets
1 teaspoon oregano
2 lemons
3 tablespoons olive oil
salt and pepper

Season the cutlets with salt, pepper and a pinch of oregano. Brush with oil and cook on a well-heated barbecue or under the grill, turning once or twice. Serve straight from the fire, with French fries, salad or *tzatzíki*, and lemon wedges.

Lamb, roasted with oil and oregano (*arnáki ladhorígani sto fóurno*)

1 kg (2 lb) leg of lamb
1 cup olive oil
juice of 1 or 2 lemons
1 tablespoon oregano
salt and pepper

Wash and dry the lamb. Season with salt, pepper and oregano. Place in a roasting pan and pour over the oil and lemon juice. Cook in a pre-heated moderate oven. As it begins to cook, pour one cup of warm water into the pan. Baste frequently. Cooking time is 1-1½ hours. Serve with roast potatoes and salad.

Lamb, roasted with potatoes (*arní me patátes*)

1 leg of lamb
1kg (2lb) potatoes
juice of 1 lemon
3 tablespoons butter
1 tablespoon oregano
salt and pepper

Wash and dry the lamb and season with salt and pepper. Place in a roasting pan. Wash and peel the potatoes. Cut into wedges and arrange around the lamb. Season with salt, pepper, oregano and lemon juice. Place a little butter on each. Pour one cup of water into the pan and roast in a pre-heated moderate oven. Allow half an hour per ½kg (1lb) of lamb.

Meat-balls (*keftédhes*)

1kg (2lb) minced veal (or mixed veal and pork)
¼kg (½lb) stale bread
1 onion, grated or finely chopped
2 tablespoons parsley, finely chopped
½ teaspoon dried mint
4 tablespoons olive oil
2 tablespoons vinegar
oil for frying (a good 2½cm (1in) in the bottom of the pan)

Cut off the bread crusts. Dip the bread in water and squeeze dry. Place in a mixing bowl with the minced meat and onion and knead well together. Add the herbs, olive oil, vinegar and seasoning and mix well. If the mixture is too thick, add a little warm water to loosen it. Leave to stand for at least 15 minutes.

Form the mixture into small round balls with the hands. Heat the oil in a large saucepan until it begins to smoke. Deep fry the meat-balls a few at a time until they are well browned. Drain on kitchen paper, and serve hot.

Meat-balls with tomato sauce (*keftédhes me sáltsa domátas*)

Prepare the meat-balls as in the preceding recipe. Fry until golden.

Prepare the tomato sauce (see page 99). When the sauce is thick and creamy, put in the meat-balls and simmer together for 15 minutes. Serve with potato purée, French fries, rice or pasta.

Minced meat and rice-balls (*yiouvarlákia me sáltsa domátas*)

1kg (2lb) minced meat
2 large onions, grated or finely chopped
½ cup rice
6 tablespoons chopped parsley
½kg (1lb) ripe tomatoes, peeled and sliced or 1 tablespoon tomato paste diluted in 2 cups of water
½ cup butter
salt and pepper

Pass the tomatoes through a coarse sieve. Melt the butter in a large saucepan. Add the tomatoes or the diluted paste, and cook over moderate heat for 10 minutes. Put the minced meat, rice, onions, half the parsley and seasoning in a mixing bowl and knead together until well blended. If the mixture is too stiff, add a little warm water. Shape the mixture into round balls the size of a small walnut and place carefully in the saucepan with the sauce. Sprinkle with the remaining oregano. Add salt and pepper and some warm water, if necessary, so that the sauce just covers the *yiouvarlákia*. Simmer gently for about 45 minutes or until most of the sauce has been absorbed. Serve with rice.

Pork chops, grilled (*brizóles hirinés sti skára*)

4 pork chops
⅓ cup olive oil
juice of ½ lemon
salt and pepper

Pound the chops a little to flatten them. Cut off any excess fat, wash and pat dry. Season with salt and pepper. Cook under heated grill or on a barbecue, basting with oil, lemon and oregano sauce. Serve with French fries and salad.

Shish kebab (*souvlákia*)

1kg (2lb) lean lamb, veal or pork
6-8 bay leaves
4 tomatoes, quartered
3 onions, quartered
3 tablespoons olive oil
juice of ½ lemon
1 teaspoon oregano
salt and pepper

Cut the meat into cubes about 2½cm (1in) thick. Skewer alternating pieces of meat, tomato, onion and bay leaf. Place in a deep dish and pour over the oil and lemon juice combined in a sauce. Season with salt and pepper and oregano. Leave to marinate for an hour.

Cook on a barbecue or under the grill, turning and basting frequently. About 3 minutes each side should be sufficient under the grill, slightly longer on a barbecue. They should not be overdone. Serve straight from the fire with a salad, and lemon wedges to squeeze over the meat.

Veal casserole with onions (*moshári stifádho*)

1 kg (2 lb) tender beef, rump or shoulder
1 kg (2 lb) small onions
4 tablespoons olive oil or butter
2-3 large ripe tomatoes, peeled and chopped
1 cup tomato juice
2 tablespoons wine vinegar
1/3 cup brandy
2-3 cloves garlic
2 bayleaves
1/2 teaspoon allspice
1/3 teaspoon cinnamon
pinch of oregano
2 cloves
1/2 cup of olive oil for frying onions
salt and black pepper

Cut the meat into 2½cm (1in) cubes. Wash and pat dry. Heat four tablespoons of oil or butter in a large saucepan and sauté the meat together with one sliced onion. When the meat begins to brown, add the tomatoes, tomato juice, brandy, garlic, bayleaves, allspice, cinnamon, oregano, cloves and salt and pepper. Simmer gently, stirring occasionally, for 1-1½ hours, until the meat is quite tender, but not overdone.

Peel the onions and sauté whole in half a cup of oil until they are golden. Add them to the meat together with their oil and the vinegar. Cook together for another 15 minutes. Serve with rice or potatoes and a green salad.

Veal casserole with tomato sauce (*moshári kokinistó*)

1 kg (2 lb) veal
3-4 tomatoes, peeled, chopped and seeded
1 onion, sliced
1 cup olive oil
1/3 cup non-resinated white wine
salt and pepper

Cut the beef into 8-10 pieces. Wash and drain. Brown the onion lightly in the heated olive oil. Add the pieces of veal. As they begin to brown, add the tomatoes, salt and pepper. Turn the ingredients over a few times with a wooden spoon. Add 2-3 cups water and simmer until the meat is tender and the sauce has thickened. Cooking time is 1-1½ hours. Serve with rice, potatoes or macaroni.

Veal chops, grilled (*brizóles mosharísies*)

4 beef chops
1/3 cup olive oil
juice of 1/2 lemon
1/2 teaspoon oregano
salt and pepper

Wash the chops and remove any excess fat. Pound the meat well and brush with a little oil, season with pepper and oregano and leave to stand for half an hour.

Salt, and cook under a very hot grill or on a very hot barbecue, so the juices are quickly sealed in. Baste frequently with oil and lemon juice. Serve with French fries or potato purée and a salad.

DESSERTS AND COFFEE

Strictly speaking there is no such thing as a Greek dessert. The Greeks finish their meals with fruit. In this section we have described some of the commoner ways of presenting fruit, other than plain. Obviously you could easily invent others for yourself. We have also included recipes for making three of the best known Greek sweets or *gliká*, even though, again, the Greeks themselves rarely eat them as desserts. The last part of the section explains the arcane art of making Turkish coffee.

Apples with cinnamon (*míla me kanéla*)

3 large apples
ground cinnamon

Wash, peel, quarter and slice the apples. Arrange the slices on a serving dish and sprinkle with cinnamon to taste. Serve immediately.

Baklavás

1/2kg (1lb) walnuts, blanched and finely chopped
1/2kg (1lb) fílo *pastry sheets*
2 cups sugar
1 cup butter
1 cup honey
2 teaspoons ground cinnamon
1 teaspoon lemon juice

Combine one cup of sugar, the cinnamon and walnuts in a bowl. Grease a baking dish with melted butter and line with three or four sheets of *fílo*, brushing the top one with melted butter. Spread a thin layer of sugar and walnut mixture over the pastry. Cover with another two sheets of *fílo*, brush with butter and spread over one more layer of filling. Continue to build up alternate layers of pastry and nut filling, until all the filling has been used. Then cover with the remaining pastry sheets and brush the top one with melted butter. Bake in a moderate oven for about one hour until golden brown.

In the meantime prepare the syrup by boiling together one cup of water, the honey, lemon juice and remaining sugar. When all the ingredients are well blended together, pour the syrup over the *baklavás* and leave to cool and absorb the syrup. To serve, cut into squares or diamonds.

Crème caramel (*kréma karamelé*)

1l (2pt) milk
2 cups sugar
6 eggs
¼ teaspoon vanilla
¼ cup water
1 teaspoon lemon juice

Pour one cup of sugar, the water and lemon juice into a small pan. Cook over low heat, stirring all the time, until the colour turns chestnut. Remove from the heat and add five tablespoons of cold water and mix well. Pour the caramel into individual moulds and toss gently to coat the moulds.

Pour the milk, vanilla and remaining sugar into a clean saucepan. Warm slowly, stirring all the while, until the mixture comes to the boil, remove from the heat. Allow to cool, and when it has become lukewarm, fold in the eggs. Pour the mixture into the moulds. Place the moulds in a baking dish. Pour round two cups of water and cook in a pre-heated moderate oven for 45 minutes. Serve cold.

Halvás

2 cups semolina
1 cup butter
3 cups milk
2½ cups sugar
½ cup blanched and peeled almonds
3 sticks cinnamon
2-3 cloves
peel of 1 lemon
ground cinnamon

Cut the almonds lengthwise into thin slices. Melt the butter in a large saucepan and when it begins to brown, add the semolina and cook for 3-4 minutes, stirring continuously with a wooden spoon. Pour in the almonds and brown.

In another saucepan, combine the milk, two cups of water, the sugar and spices. Bring to the boil and cook together for just two minutes. Remove the cloves and cinnamon sticks and pour into the semolina mixture while still very hot. Cook over low heat for 3 minutes, stirring all the time. Remove from the heat. Cover the pan with a clean cloth and allow to stand for 5 minutes.

Serve sprinkled with cinnamon.

Honey puffs (*loukoumádhes*)

5 cups plain flour
1 tablespoon yeast
1 teaspoon salt
2 cups sugar
1 cup honey
ground cinnamon

Dissolve the yeast in a cup of lukewarm water. Pour the flour into a large mixing bowl, add the yeast and mix with a wooden spoon, adding sufficient water to make a thick soft dough. Knead well, cover, and leave to stand in a warm place for at least 3 hours, until the mixture has doubled in volume and bubbles begin to appear on the surface.

Bring one cup of water to the boil and add sugar and honey. Cook together until the mixture acquires the consistency of syrup.

Heat about 2½cm (1in) of olive oil in a deep saucepan. When it is very hot, drop in spoonfuls of dough and cook until golden. Rinse the spoon in cold water between each spoonful to prevent the dough sticking. Drain the dollops of dough well and heap together on a serving dish. Pour over the syrup and sprinkle with cinnamon and serve immediately.

Peaches with sugar (*rodhákina me záhari*)

1kg (2lb) ripe firm peaches
3-4 tablespoons sugar

Blanch and peel the peaches. Split in two, and remove the stones. Cut the flesh into wedges. Arrange on a serving dish, sprinkle with sugar and leave in the fridge for at least one hour before serving.

Rice pudding (*rizógalo*)

1l (2pt) milk
½ cup short-grain rice
2 tablespoons corn flour, mixed with 2 tablespoons water
4 tablespoons sugar
¼ teaspoon vanilla
ground cinnamon
salt

Pour the rice, a pinch of salt and one cup of water into a heavy-bottomed saucepan. Bring to the boil and cook until all the water has been absorbed. Add the milk, sugar and corn flour. Cook over low heat, stirring all the time, until the rice is soft and the milk creamy. Remove from the heat. Add the vanilla, mix and pour into small individual bowls. Serve warm or cold, sprinkled with cinnamon.

Strawberry dessert (*fráoules*)

1kg (2lb) just ripe strawberries
lemon juice
3-4 tablespoons sugar

Wash the strawberries and drain well. Remove the stems, slice in two and place in a serving bowl. Sprinkle with lemon juice and sugar and toss gently. Leave to marinate in the fridge for at least one hour before serving.

Yoghurt with honey and walnuts (*yiaóurti me méli ke karídhia*)

½kg (1lb) thick strained yoghurt
4 tablespoons honey
4 tablespoons coarsely chopped walnuts

Place the yoghurt in individual shallow pudding bowls. Pour over the honey and walnuts and serve.

This is the most typical Greek dessert, but yoghurt goes well with most fruit and nuts and you can easily try your own combinations, with or without honey as well.

COFFEE

Turkish coffee, or Greek coffee as it is now called because of Greek animosity towards the Turks, is drunk throughout the day. The natural assumption of most café waiters is that when a foreigner orders coffee he wants instant coffee, which the Greeks call *neskafé* whether it is Nescafé or any other brand. But if you really want Turkish coffee, then you have to ask for *elinikós kafés*, i.e. Greek coffee. It is not as confusing as it sounds!

Greek coffee is always served with a glass of cold water, which you drink first, to clear the system. It is made in a special little conical pot with a long handle called a *bríki* and drunk in very small cups. Don't try to drink the dark mud of grounds that always remain at the bottom.

It is not difficult to make, despite the fact that the old-time connoisseurs claim there are 40 different ways of doing it. There are basically three methods nowadays: sugarless or *skétos*, medium-sweet or *métrios*, and sweet – *glikós*. After you have tried your hand at it a few times, you will see that the end product depends not only on the amount of coffee and sugar you use, but also on how the coffee is prepared, how often you stir it, how quickly it cooks, whether it is allowed to boil and so on. As a general rule, the slower it cooks the better.

Medium-sweet Greek coffee (*métrios kafés*)

1 small coffee cup lukewarm water
1 heaped teaspoon Turkish ground coffee
1 level teaspoon sugar

Put the water, sugar and coffee in a *bríki*. Heat slowly, stirring only once. When bubbles begin to rise to the surface, withdraw from the heat and stir again. Return to the heat until the coffee begins to froth, and remove before it boils. If you don't like froth (*kaïmáki*) on your coffee, allow it to boil.

To make a *glikós kafés*, double the amount of sugar. To make *skétos*, omit the sugar altogether.

Kafé frapé

A fairly recent Greek invention, *kafé frapé* makes a very refreshing summer drink. In Greece it is always made with Nescafé, but you can just as well use any other brand.

1 heaped teaspoon instant coffee
½ glass cold water
3-4 ice cubes
milk and sugar (optional)

Put the coffee in a shaker and dilute with just one teaspoon of warm water. Add the cold water and ice cubes, and milk and sugar to taste, Shake vigorously for 5 seconds. Serve immediately, topped with plenty of froth.

Weights and Measures

The metric system is used for all measurements in Greece now, which is why we have put metric measurements first in the recipes, with the *avoir du poids* weight in parentheses. We have, in fact, simplified the equivalence of 1 lb by calling 1 kilo 2 lb, ½ kilo 1 lb and ¼ kilo ½ lb. This is not strictly accurate as you will see from the table below. But the difference is small, and you will find it much easier to think in round terms when asking the shopkeeper for *éna kiló* (1 kg), *misó kiló* (½ kg) and so on. Besides, Greek cooking recipes do not require absolute precision, and no Greek cooks can ever agree about the exact proportions for various dishes.

EQUIVALENT MEASUREMENTS

Dry and solid measures

Grams	Oz.
30	1
113	4
170	6
225	8 (½ lb)
450	1 lb
675	1½ lb
900	2 lb
1 kg	2 lb 3 oz

Liquid measures

The Greeks express volumes in litres: 1 litre is about 1¾ pints. For ease of conversion, it is accurate enough to think of 1 litre as 2 pints and ½ litre as 1 pint.

Although the official metric measurement of volume is litres, and that is what you will find printed on bottles and tins in Greece, the Greeks very often talk about kilos. When, for example, you order your wine from the barrel, you ask for *éna kiló* (1 kg) or *misó kiló* (½kg); 1 kilo is exactly the same measurement as 1 litre. The references to cups and half cups in the recipe section equal a regular tea cup. Again this does not require absolute precision.

Oven temperatures

The following table shows Fahrenheit and Centigrade equivalents.

Low	300°F	150°C
Moderate	357°F	190°C
Hot	425°F	220°C
Very Hot	475°F	250°C

Glossary

Here is an English-Greek vocabulary which will help you in shopping for food and household goods. Don't be shy about not speaking grammatically. People will soon understand you. Besides, nothing creates a better relationship quicker than when a foreigner tries to speak the language of the country. Even if you only say *kaliméra* (good day) and *adío* (goodbye), it will be appreciated. Of course, if you are interested in learning to speak Greek properly, then you will need to buy a specialised language book.

The most important thing in pronouncing Greek words is to put the stress in the right place. We have marked the stressed syllable in every word with an acute accent,´.

As for the sounds, if you say them as we have written them in English characters, you won't go too far wrong. Remember that in Greek you say every letter; there are no silent ones as in English. And notice the following differences: *ou* sounds like *oo* in *food*; *h* like *ch* in *loch*; *th* like *th* in *thin*; *dh* like *th* in *then*. And *r* is always pronounced with a slight roll.

Fruit	*fróuta*
apples	*míla*
apricots	*veríkoka*
bananas	*banánes*
cherries	*kerásia*
figs	*síka*
grapes	*stafília*
lemons	*lemónia*
lioquats	*móusmoula*
melons	*pepónia*
nectarines	*nektarínia*
oranges	*portokália*
peaches	*rodhákina/yermádhes*
pears	*ahládhia*
plums	*korómila/vanílies*
pomegranates	*ródhia*
strawberries	*fráoules*
tangerines	*mandarínia*
watermelons	*karpóuzia*

Herbs and spices

allspice	*bahári*
aniseed	*glikániso*
basil	*vasilikós*
bay	*dháfni*
caper	*kápari*
chamomile	*hamomíli*
cinnamon	*kanéla*
clove	*garífalo*
dill	*ánithos*
fennel	*máratho*
lime flowers	*tílio*
marjoram	*mantzouràna*
mint	*dhiósmos*
mountain tea	*tsáï tou vounóu*
nutmeg	*moshokáridho*
oregano	*rígani*
parsley	*maïdanó*
rocket	*róka*
rosemary	*dhendrolívano*
sage	*faskómilo*
savory	*thróumbi*
thyme	*thimári*

Meat and poultry — *kréas, pouleriká*

beef	*vódhino*
breast	*stíthos*
chicken	*kotópoulo*
chops	*brizóles*
goat	*yídha*
kid	*katsíki*
kidneys	*nefrá*
lamb	*arnáki*
lamb cutlets	*païdhákia*
leg	*bóuti*
liver	*sikóti*
minced meat	*kimá*
mutton	*arní*
pork	*hirinó*
rump	*kilóto*
shoulder	*spála*
veal	*moshári*

Nuts and seeds	*xirí karpí*
almonds	*amígdhala*
chestnuts	*kástana*
hazel nuts	*foundóukia*
marrow seeds	*pasatémbo*
pine nuts	*koukounária*
pistachios	*fistíkia*
walnuts	*karídhia*

Seafood and fish	*thalasiná, psária*
anchovy	*gávros*
bogue	*gópa*
cockles	*kidhónia*
cod	*bakaliáros*
cuttlefish	*soupiá*
dentex	*sinagrídha*
gilt-head bream	*tsipóura*
lobster	*astakós*
mackerel	*skoubrí*
mussels	*mídhia*
octopus	*ohtapódhi*
oysters	*strídhia*
pandora	*lithríni*
picarel	*marídhes*
prawns	*garídhes*
prawns/scampi	*karavídhes*
red mullet	*barbóuni*
sardines	*sardhéles*
sea bass	*lavráki*
sea bream	*fangrí*
sea urchins	*ahiní*
sole	*glósa*
squid	*kalamári*
swordfish	*xifía*
two-banded bream	*sargós*

Vegetables	*láhana*
artichokes	*anginámes*
aubergines/eggplant	*melitzánes*
beans: black-eyed	*mavromátika*
bobby or French	*fasolákia*
butter	*yígandes*
haricot	*fasólia*

beetroot	*padzária*
cabbage	*láhano*
carrots	*karóta*
cauliflower	*kounoupídhi*
celery	*sélino*
courgettes/zucchini	*kolokíthia*
cucumber	*angóuri*
garlic	*skórdho*
greens	*hórta*
leeks	*prása*
lettuce (Cos)	*maróuli*
okra	*bámies*
onions	*kremídhia*
peas	*arakás*
peppers	*piperiés*
potatoes	*patátes*
spinach	*spanáki*
tomatoes	*domátes*

Shops and shopping

bakery	*fóurnos*
bank	*trápeza*
beer	*bíra*
biscuits	*biskóta*
brandy	*koniák*
bread	*psomí*
butcher	*hasápis*
butcher's shop	*hasápiko*
butter	*vóutiro*
cafe	*kafenío*
cakes	*kéïk*
charcoal	*kárvouna*
cheese	*tirí*
chemist's shop	*farmakío*
coffee	*kafés*
cream	*kréma*
currants	*mávres stafídhes*
dustbin bags	*sakóules ya skoupídhia*
eggs	*avgá*
fishmonger	*ihthiopolío*
flour	*alévri*
flour, self-raising	*alévri pou fouskóni*
grams	*gramária*
100 grams	*ekató gramária*
150 grams	*ekatón penínda gramária*

200 grams	*dhiakósia gramária*
greengrocer	*manávis*
greengrocer's shop	*manáviko*
grocer	*bakális*
grocer's shop	*bakáliko*
honey	*méli*
icecream	*pagotó*
jam	*marmeládha*
kilo/ 1 kilo	*éna kiló*
½ kilo	*misó kiló*
¼ kilo	*éna tétarto*
2 kilos	*dhío kilá*
lemonade	*lemonádha*
market	*agorá*
milk	*gála*
olives	*eliés*
olive oil	*ládhi*
orangeade	*portokaládha*
paper napkins	*hartopetsétes*
patisserie	*zaharoplastío*
pepper	*pipéri*
Post Office	*tahidhromío*
rice	*rízi*
rusks	*paximádhia*
salt	*aláti*
spaghetti	*makarónia*
sugar	*záhari*
sultanas	*stafídhes*
tea	*tsáï*
toilet paper	*hartí iyias*
vinegar	*xídhi*
water	*neró*
water, boiled	*neró emfialoméno*
wine	*krasí*

In the kitchen

baking dish	*tapsí*
cooker	*kouzína*
cup	*flitzáni*
electric	*ilektrikó*
fork	*piróuni*
fridge	*psiyío*
frying pan	*tigáni*
fuse	*asfália*
gas	*gázi*

glass	*potíri*
kitchen	*kouzína*
knife	*mahéri*
light bulb	*lámba*
matches	*spírta*
plate	*piáto*
plug (electrical)	*fís*
power-point	*príza*
saucepan	*katsaróla*
spoon	*koutáli*

Other useful words and phrases

a few	*lígo*
a little	*lígo*
a lot	*polí*
big	*megálo*
bill	*logariasmós*
bottle	*boukáli*
bottle opener/can-opener	*anihtíri*
box	*koutí*
change (money)	*résta*
cheap	*ftinó*
clean	*katharó*
closed	*klistó*
dirty	*vrómiko*
dry-cleaner	*stegnokathartstírio*
empty	*ádhio*
enough	*arketá*
expensive	*akrivó*
food	*faí*
fresh	*frésko*
full	*yemáto*
good-morning, good-day	*kaliméra*
goodbye	*adío*
heavy	*varí*
how much	*póso?*
less	*pió lígo*
light	*elafró*
money	*leftá*
more	*akóma*
no	*óhi*
nothing	*típota*
not very	*óhi polí*
old (food)	*sápio*
open	*aniktó*

please	*parakaló*
ready	*étimo*
ripe	*órimo*
small	*mikró*
sour	*xinó*
sweet	*glikó*
thank you	*efharistó*
tinned food	*konsérva*
today	*símera*
tomorrow	*ávrio*
too little	*polí lígo*
too much	*pára polí*
unripe	*ágouro*
very	*polí*
yes	*ne*
yesterday	*ehthés*

A few phrases

The simplest way to ask for something is to start with *parakaló*, which means 'if you please'. For example 'Do you have any apples?' would be '*Parakaló, éhete míla?*'. 'Can I have a kilo of minced meat?' is '*Parakaló, éna kiló kimá?*'

What is this?	*ti íne aftó?*
How much does it cost?	*póso káni?*
How much does a kilo cost?	*póso káni to kiló?*

Some numerals

one	*éna*
two	*dhío*
three	*tría*
four	*tésera*
five	*pénde*
six	*éxi*
seven	*eftá*
eight	*októ*
nine	*eniá*
ten	*dhéka*
eleven	*éndheka*
twelve	*dhódheka*
thirteen	*dhekatría*
fourteen	*dhekatésera*
fifteen	*dhekapénde*
sixteen	*dhekaéxi*

seventeen	*dhekaeftá*
eighteen	*dhekaoktó*
nineteen	*dhekaeniá*
twenty	*íkosi*
thirty	*triánda*
forty	*saránda*
fifty	*penínda*
sixty	*exínda*
seventy	*evdhomínda*
eighty	*ogdhónda*
ninety	*enenínda*
one hundred	*ekató*
five hundred	*pendakósia*
one thousand	*hílía*
two thousand	*dhío hiliádhes*

Bibliography

Davidson, Alan, *Mediterranean Seafood*, Penguin Books Ltd, Harmondsworth, 1981.

Huxley, Anthony, and Taylor, William, *Flowers of Greece and the Aegean*, Chatto and Windus Ltd, London, 1977.

Kapsaskis, Angeline, *The Commonsense Greek Cookery Book*, Angus & Robertson Publishers, North Ryde, NSW, Australia, 1977.

Mark, Theonie, *Greek Islands Cooking*, B.T. Batsford Ltd, London, 1978.

Paradisi, Chrisa, *Megali Mayiriki Zaharoplastiki*, Fivos, Athens, 1976.

Petropoulos, Elias, *O Tourkikos Kafes en Elladhi*, Grammata, Athens, 1979.

Salaman, Rena, *Greek Food*, Fontana Paperbacks, London, 1983.

Skoura, Sophia, *I Nea Mayiriki*, Tipos A.E., Athens, 1979.

Stubbs, Joyce M., *The Home Book of Greek Cookery*, Faber and Faber, London, 1974.

Theoharous, Anne, *Cooking the Greek Way*, Magnum Books, London, 1979.

Index

NOTES

NOTES

NOTES

NOTES

NOTES